THE BRASS BUTTERFLY

To

ALASTAIR SIM

in gratitude and affection

By the same author

LORD OF THE FLIES
THE INHERITORS
PINCHER MARTIN
FREE FALL
THE SPIRE
THE PYRAMID
THE SCORPION GOD: THREE SHORT NOVELS
DARKNESS VISIBLE
RITES OF PASSAGE
THE PAPER MEN
THE HOT GATES, AND OTHER OCCASIONAL PIECES
A MOVING TARGET
AN EGYPTIAN JOURNAL
CLOSE QUARTERS

THE BRASS
BUTTERFLY
A Play in Three Acts

WILLIAM GOLDING

faber and faber
LONDON · BOSTON

First published in 1958
by Faber and Faber Limited
3 Queen Square, London WC1N 3AU
First published in this edition 1969
Reprinted 1970, 1971 and 1975
Reissued 1987
Printed in Great Britain by
Redwood Burn Ltd, Trowbridge, Wiltshire
All rights reserved

© by William Gerald Golding 1958

ISBN 0 571 09073 7 (Faber Paperbacks)
ISBN 0 571 05470 6 (hard bound edition)

CHARACTERS

MAMILLIUS
CAPTAIN OF THE GUARD
POSTUMUS
EMPEROR
PHANOCLES
EUPHROSYNE
SERGEANT
ATTENDANTS, ETC.

The first performance in Great Britain of
THE BRASS BUTTERFLY was given at the
New Theatre, Oxford, on 24th February 1958.
It was directed by Alastair Sim. The setting
was designed by Edward Seago and the cos-
tumes and furniture by Hutchinson Scott.
The cast was as follows:

MAMILLIUS	Jeremy Spenser
CAPTAIN	Jack Hedley
POSTUMUS	George Selway
EMPEROR	Alastair Sim
PHANOCLES	George Cole
EUPHROSYNE	Eileen Moore
SERGEANT	Geoffrey Matthews

ATTENDANTS, SLAVES, ETC.: Stella Brett,
Gillian Muir, Pauline Sutton, Hendrik
Baker, Ron Scott-Dodd, Michael Gartred,
Maitland Moss

ACT I

Scene I. *The* EMPEROR'S *villa on the island of Capri.*

Everything is on a large scale but in exquisite good taste. Perhaps the taste is the least bit too good—in any case the bust of a young and brutal-looking man, Back centre, is noticeable as the only sign of an exterior world where life is earnest, real and rather bloody-minded. The bust stands under an opening to the sky.

Entrances: *Right, to depths of villa. Left, to the open.*

Architect has cunningly suggested on the inside here, what a magnificent front door the EMPEROR *has to his summer cottage. Bright sunlight.*

Time: *Late afternoon some time in the third century* A.D. *No one is going to be more specific. It is an unspecific-looking place, except for the bust.*

MAMILLIUS, *a man-boy?—is lying on his stomach on a couch Right centre. He is in the throes of literary composition.*

MAMILLIUS: "Darken the five bright windows of my mind,
          My soul is stretched out rigid in her bed.
          Admit the corpse within. Pull down the blind—"
          Pull down the blind . . .
          (*Sees bust—Springs up, flings cloak over it and returns to the couch.*)
          "Admit the corpse within. Pull down the blind."
          Pull down—pull down the blind—
          (*Pause. Then inspiration comes.*)
          "How *long*—"
          (OFFICER OF THE GUARD *is heard shouting, off.*)
OFFICER: Halt. Into line. Left turn. By the right—dress!
          Guard and men with arms—order—arms! Stand
          at—ease!
          (CAPTAIN OF THE GUARD *comes in, left. Halts.*

Draws his sword. Stands easy. MAMILLIUS *pretends he is alone, but each time he paces towards the door the* CAPTAIN *comes to attention and reverts to at-ease as he turns away.*)

MAMILLIUS: Tell me, Captain, must we continue to play this foolish game?

CAPTAIN: Game, sir?

MAMILLIUS: Moving your feet like that.

CAPTAIN: It's not a game, sir. Regulations.

MAMILLIUS: And without regulations the empire would totter.

CAPTAIN: Yes, sir.

MAMILLIUS: That would be exciting at least.

CAPTAIN: Yes, sir.

MAMILLIUS: I am new to the imperial scene, Captain. Tell me, do you jump about just so when my grandfather comes near you?

CAPTAIN: Oh no, sir. We stand to attention whenever the Emperor comes in sight.

MAMILLIUS: And when General Postumus—(*looking at cloak on bust which he has forgotten and which he now removes with elaborate unconcern*)—and when General Postumus comes in sight?

CAPTAIN: No, sir. Twenty paces for General Postumus— but we extend it a bit for the General, since he takes such a personal interest in discipline.

MAMILLIUS: I am neither the Emperor nor General Postumus; just make yourself as comfortable as that dreary uniform will allow you.

CAPTAIN: Sorry, sir. Regulations. Distance makes no difference now. "Whilst addressed by a member of the Imperial Family officers of the guard will remain at attention until dismissed or until the Imperial Personage indicates beyond all reasonable doubt that the officer is no longer the subject of his interest."

MAMILLIUS: How bored I am! How bored you must be!

CAPTAIN: No, sir. Used to it.

MAMILLIUS: There's only one Imperial Family.

CAPTAIN: Yes, sir. But the regulations are the same in the vicinity of the vestal virgins and at public executions.

MAMILLIUS: So I'm an Imperial Personage.

CAPTAIN: Yes, sir. Just, sir.

MAMILLIUS: Only just? How near do I have to come before you give that horrid little jump?

CAPTAIN: Five paces, sir.

MAMILLIUS: Because I'm a bastard?

CAPTAIN: (*shocked*). Oh no, sir. You're not a bastard, sir. You're the Emperor's illegitimate grandson, sir.

MAMILLIUS: Tell me, how does an Imperial Personage dismiss an officer?

CAPTAIN: The Emperor does it with one finger, like that, sir. Sorry, sir. I'm not here for you. I had to turn out the guard because General Postumus is coming to say good-bye to the Emperor. You're just an accident, sir.

MAMILLIUS: A what?

CAPTAIN: Oh—er—what I meant was—well—I certainly didn't mean what you probably thought I meant. (*Sees Postumus approaching.*) Excuse me, sir. Guard and men with arms! Shun! Slope arms! (ENTER POSTUMUS.)

POSTUMUS: (*To Captain*). Take up position with the guard and stand them at ease.

CAPTAIN: Sir. (*Salutes and exits. Voice off*) Guard. Order arms! Stand at ease! Keep still in the back there.

POSTUMUS: Did you put him up to it?

MAMILLIUS: If you are talking about the Captain, he gets everything out of a book, Postumus.

POSTUMUS: I'm not talking about the Captain, you young fool. This other business. Someone let them get away. Did you do it?

MAMILLIUS: I'm too bored to do anything.

POSTUMUS: Give me a straight answer! (*Seizes his wrist.*) Did you help them escape or not?

MAMILLIUS: Let me go! Let me go! I shall go back to Sybaris.

9

I shall complain to grandfather. I warn you, Postumus. I warn you.

POSTUMUS: Don't think you'll get away with it, Mamillius. I know what sort of influence you've got with him—

MAMILLIUS: A civilizing influence. Grandfather!

(ENTER THE EMPEROR ATTENDED.)

EMPEROR: Ah, there you are, Postumus. Saying good-bye to Mamillius? I'm so glad you get on well together. Come and sit for a moment, and drink wine with me.

POSTUMUS: Caesar—(*Emperor halts him with a gesture and signs slaves to leave*). Someone gave them a boat. Who was it? Did he?

MAMILLIUS: I haven't got a boat.

EMPEROR: No, of course he hasn't. Would you like one?

POSTUMUS: Caesar!

EMPEROR: He doesn't understand, you know. Mamillius, a dreadful thing has happened. The ends of justice have been thwarted.

POSTUMUS: And I've been made to look a fool.

EMPEROR: Nothing could do that. Nothing shall do that. You are my Heir Designate, Postumus. Take your fleet to Tripoli and extend the Empire. Go and give the blessing of civilization to the Sahara.

POSTUMUS: I shall do so, and hope to show myself worthy of the imperial inheritance. But these three men—I must be certain that my work here is completed.

EMPEROR: The Heir Designate, Mamillius, pausing here at Capri to pay his respects to the Emperor, since the wind was contrary, occupied some days in examining the Imperial Household for disaffected persons, of whom he found three.

POSTUMUS: The executions should have taken place this afternoon.

EMPEROR: But they got away.

MAMILLIUS: What was their crime?

POSTUMUS: They were Christians.

10

EMPEROR: Postumus is about the only man left to keep up the good old Roman customs.

MAMILLIUS: Why should he think I had anything to do with it? Christianity is horribly vulgar. I do not care for vulgarity.

POSTUMUS: After the orders I gave, only a member of the Imperial Household could have got them a boat.

MAMILLIUS: Perhaps they simply stole one.

EMPEROR: They would hardly do that, do you think?

POSTUMUS: And therefore I can only conclude—

MAMILLIUS: —that *I* gave them one?
(POSTUMUS *rises*.)

EMPEROR: (*intervening*). Postumus, the boy has only just heard about your Christians.

POSTUMUS: Where has he been these last two days?

EMPEROR: In Arcadia with the Muse of poetry. Postumus, you and I know so much more than he. We live in a different world—the real one. Accept my assurances to quieten the thought lurking in your head. The boy is, and will remain, a private person. Eh, Mamillius?

MAMILLIUS: Yes, grandfather.

EMPEROR: He cares nothing for public affairs—does he, Mamillius?

MAMILLIUS: No, grandfather.

EMPEROR: Have I ever deceived you, Postumus?

POSTUMUS: Yes.

EMPEROR: But in matters of moment?

POSTUMUS: Perhaps not. Or if you have, Caesar, you have concealed it very cleverly.

EMPEROR: Come, Postumus, you are too intelligent to be deceived; so you may accept my assurances.
(*Pause*)

POSTUMUS: (*suddenly*). Contrary wind or not, I must be going, or there will be none of the season left.

EMPEROR: You accept my word then?

POSTUMUS: I have your interests at heart—

EMPEROR: Because they are your interests too.

11

POSTUMUS: Let the boy remain your companion so long as he becomes nothing more important.

EMPEROR: Surely.

POSTUMUS: And find out who gave those Christians a boat.

EMPEROR: The enquiry could not be in safer hands. Good-bye, my dear Heir Designate. Come back with the usual laurels on your sword.

POSTUMUS: I shall try to do so.

EMPEROR: A last cup before you go?

POSTUMUS: No, no.

EMPEROR: Good-bye then. Our thoughts go with you and your gallant men. And remember, Postumus, I shall keep you informed of everything that happens.

POSTUMUS: I shall keep myself informed. For the time being, good-bye, Caesar.

(EXIT POSTUMUS.)

EMPEROR: Good-bye! Good-bye!

OFFICER: (*off*). Guard shun! Slope arms! Present—arms!

(FANFARE)

EMPEROR: Good-bye! Good-bye! Death or victory! But victory for choice, of course!

OFFICER: (*off*). Slope—arms! Order arms! Turning right—dismiss!

EMPEROR: That was an affecting moment, eh, Mamillius? Good-bye! Good-bye!

OFFICER: (*distant*). Present—arms!

(FANFARE)

EMPEROR: My blessing etcetera. Good-bye! How many today? (*Turning to petitions*) Watch him go, Mamillius. It is a splendid ritual. Watch him, Mamillius. Mamillius!

MAMILLIUS: (*sulkily*). Caesar?

EMPEROR: Report his progress, will you? You might wave once or twice. Try to combine affectionate regret with boyish impetuosity.

MAMILLIUS: The Heir Designate is about to step down to the quay.

12

OFFICER: (*very distant*). Present—arms!
(FANFARE *distant*)

EMPEROR: It is very trying to a man of any musical sensibility to have to hear that same old fanfare over and over again. Not that Postumus minds, you know. So long as the instruments are all at the same angle he is perfectly happy.

MAMILLIUS: The Heir Designate is about to go aboard a boat.

EMPEROR: Why are you not waving?

MAMILLIUS: Why should I?

EMPEROR: Come away then, and let me.
(EMPEROR *gives some last courtly waves.*)
There. I think that will do. And now for these petitions. Will you help me?

MAMILLIUS: I looked at some. They bore me.

EMPEROR: They bore me, too. Forget him now, Mamillius. Postumus will be gone a long time.

MAMILLIUS: I shan't feel easy till he's off the island. There. At last he's seated in the boat.

EMPEROR: That will take him out to the fleet. How peaceful everything is!

MAMILLIUS: Too peaceful.

EMPEROR: Already? Let me think how you can be amused.
(*He lifts a finger. In the villa a* EUNUCH *begins to sing.* MAMILLIUS *listens for a while.*)

MAMILLIUS: No.
(EMPEROR *switches off* EUNUCH.)
Even your famous singing eunuch is not what he was.

EMPEROR: (*drily*). He would agree with you, Mamillius.

MAMILLIUS: Is there an imperial recipe for the cure of boredom?

EMPEROR: Millions of people must think that an emperor's grandson—even one on the left-hand side—is utterly happy.

MAMILLIUS: I have run through the sources of happiness.

EMPEROR: An hour ago you were eager to help me with these petitions.

MAMILLIUS: That was before I had begun to read them. Does the whole world think of nothing but cadging favours?

EMPEROR: Write some more of your exquisite verses. I particularly liked the ones to be inscribed on an eggshell. They appealed to the gastronome in me.

MAMILLIUS: I found someone had done it before. I shall not write on eggshells again.

EMPEROR: Try the other arts.

MAMILLIUS: Declamation? Gastronomy?

EMPEROR: You are too shy for the one and too young for the other.

MAMILLIUS: I thought you applauded my interest in cooking.

EMPEROR: You talk, Mamillius, but you do not understand. Gastronomy is not the pleasure of youth but the evocation of it.

MAMILLIUS: The Father of his Country is pleased to be obscure. And I am still bored.

EMPEROR: If you were not so wonderfully transparent I should prescribe senna.

MAMILLIUS: I am boringly regular.

EMPEROR: A woman?

MAMILLIUS: (*indignantly*). I hope I am more civilized than that! (THE EMPEROR *rocks with laughter*.) Am I so funny?

EMPEROR: I am sorry. Mamillius, you are so desperately up-to-date that you dare not enjoy yourself for fear of being thought old-fashioned.

MAMILLIUS: The trouble is, Grandfather, I do not even want to. There is nothing new under the sun. Everything has been invented, everything has been written, everything has been done.

EMPEROR: Have you ever heard of China?

MAMILLIUS: No.

EMPEROR: I must have heard of China first twenty years ago. An island, I thought, beyond India. It would take Postumus years to get there with his fleet. Since then, odd fragments of information have filtered

14

through to me. Do you know, Mamillius, that
China is an empire bigger than our own?

MAMILLIUS: That is nonsense. A contradiction in nature.

EMPEROR: But true, none the less.

MAMILLIUS: Travellers' tales.

EMPEROR: I try to prove to you how vast and exciting life is.

MAMILLIUS: I do not care to go exploring.

EMPEROR: Stay home then, and amuse an old man who grows
lonely.

MAMILLIUS: Thank you for allowing me to be your fool.

EMPEROR: Boy, go and get mixed up in a good, bloody battle!

MAMILLIUS: I leave that sort of thing to your *official* heir.
Postumus is an insensitive bruiser. He can have all
the battles he wants. Besides, a battle cheapens
life, and I find life cheap enough already.

EMPEROR: Then the Father of his Country can do nothing for
his own grandson.

MAMILLIUS: I am tired of twiddling my fingers.

EMPEROR: So soon? Have I been very foolish? Be careful,
Mamillius. A condition of our unusual friendship
is that you keep your fingers out of hot water.
Go on twiddling them. I want you to have a long
life, even if in the end you die of boredom. Do not
become ambitious.

MAMILLIUS: I am not ambitious for power.

EMPEROR: Continue to convince Postumus of that. Leave the
prospect of ruling to him. He likes it.

MAMILLIUS: Yet you would prefer—

EMPEROR: No.

MAMILLIUS: You would prefer—

EMPEROR: Be silent!

MAMILLIUS: —that I should inherit the gold fringe on your
purple toga.

EMPEROR: What place do you think this is? Have you read
no history? If his agents heard you we should
neither of us live another six months. Never
say such a thing again! It is an order! (*Pause*)
Listen.

15

MAMILLIUS: I am listening.

EMPEROR: Not to me. Do you hear nothing?

MAMILLIUS: I hear nothing. Yes, I do. Like the beating of a heart.

EMPEROR: It is indeed the beating of a heart, Mamillius—a thousand hearts. They cannot spread the sails, but Postumus is in a hurry. There is a drum in every ship and the slaves keep time to it. They are condemned to the oar as I am condemned daily to these merciless petitions. Life is not organized to make men happy, Mamillius.

MAMILLIUS: What have I to do with slaves?

EMPEROR: Nothing practical, of course; but your indifference to the idea of them argues a dislike of humanity.

MAMILLIUS: And you?

EMPEROR: I accept humanity.

MAMILLIUS: I avoid humanity.

EMPEROR: You must not do that, Mamillius. We must get Postumus to agree to my giving you a small governorship. Egypt?

MAMILLIUS: Greece, if I must.

EMPEROR: Greece is booked, I am afraid—there is even a waiting list. It is our Roman passion for second-hand culture.

MAMILLIUS: Egypt, then.

EMPEROR: A part of Egypt. If you go, Mamillius, it will be for your own sake. You would find nothing of me on your return but ashes and a monument or two. Be happy then, if only to cheer an ageing civil servant!

MAMILLIUS: What has Egypt to make me *happy*? There is nothing new, even out of Africa.

EMPEROR: Here is something new for you! They are two of your prospective subjects. You had better see them.

(MAMILLIUS *takes the petition and turns so that he can read it in the sunset light.*)

MAMILLIUS: Oh, no! It can't be! But Grandfather—what does he mean?

EMPEROR: I hoped you would explain.

MAMILLIUS: But the diagram! Grandfather, it's indecent!
(*He giggles.*)

EMPEROR: Be careful Mamillius—you are harbouring old-fashioned ideas—

MAMILLIUS: No—but look at that! Really!
(*They laugh together.*)

MAMILLIUS: Otherwise, I suppose it *could* be some sort of a ship.

EMPEROR: I get the same impression. At least this one is literate, if somewhat incoherent.

MAMILLIUS: He's mad!

EMPEROR: They are. Frequently.

MAMILLIUS: Violent?

EMPEROR: Sometimes.

MAMILLIUS: I know what he wants.

EMPEROR: What?

MAMILLIUS: He wants to play at boats with Caesar!
(*They laugh.*)

EMPEROR: Oh, very good, Mamillius— very good! Yes—he wants to play at boats! Shall we see him?

MAMILLIUS: Oh, yes please, Grandfather.

EMPEROR: Very well.
(MAMILLIUS *strikes bell.*
ENTER CAPTAIN.)

MAMILLIUS: Captain—

CAPTAIN: Sir?

MAMILLIUS: The Emperor will—what will you do, Grandfather?

EMPEROR: Grant an audience, Captain.

CAPTAIN: Caesar!
(*He takes his station behind the* EMPEROR'S *chair with sword drawn.*)

MAMILLIUS: (*coldly official*). The Emperor grants an audience to the petitioners—what are they, Grandfather?

EMPEROR: Phanocles and Euphrosyne.

17

MAMILLIUS: —to the petitioners Phanocles and Euphrosyne.

USHER: (*off*). The Emperor permits the petitioners Phanocles and Euphrosyne to approach him!

MAMILLIUS: What do I do?

EMPEROR: Show an interest in something.

(ENTER USHER. PHANOCLES *is bobbing behind him. As the* USHER *speaks* PHANOCLES *gets round him and explores the stage in search of the* EMPEROR.)

USHER: Caesar: The petitioners Phanocles and Euphrosyne!

(USHER *can find neither.*)

PHANOCLES: Caesar! Caesar!

EMPEROR: So you are Phanocles?

PHANOCLES: An Alexandrian, Caesar.

(ENTER EUPHROSYNE *balancing the model on her head.* THE USHER, *satisfied that he has now delivered both petitioners, withdraws.*)

EMPEROR: Mamillius—Mamillius!

MAMILLIUS: Caesar?

EMPEROR: Ah! I see. You are showing an interest, I believe.

MAMILLIUS: Yes, Caesar.

EMPEROR: You are guarding my chair, Captain—not eyeing my guests.

CAPTAIN: Caesar!

EMPEROR: And you, Phanocles?

PHANOCLES: Phanocles, Caesar—the son of Myron, an Alexandrian.

EMPEROR: Son of Myron? The Librarian?

PHANOCLES: Yes, Caesar.

EMPEROR: I remember him. Did your father finish his dictionary? He had reached B when I left some forty years ago.

PHANOCLES: He died seven years ago, Caesar. He reached F, but it was too much for him.

EMPEROR: And you will finish his life's work?

PHANOCLES: I was an assistant, Caesar—but then—something happened. Look at this, Caesar. (*He realizes he is without the model, then remembers, looks round, and discovers it on Euphrosyne's head. After some*

18

difficulty he manages to set it up on portable trestles.)

EMPEROR: And you want to play boats with Caesar?

PHANOCLES: There was obstruction, Caesar, from top to bottom. I was wasting my time and public money, they said, and I was dabbling in black magic, they said, and they laughed. I am a poor man, and when the last of my father's money was spent—he left me a little, you understand—not much—and when I spent that—what are we to do, Caesar? There was obstruction and mockery, incomprehension, anger, persecution—

EMPEROR: How much did it cost you to see me today?

PHANOCLES: Three pieces of gold.

EMPEROR: That seems reasonable. I am not in Rome.

PHANOCLES: It was all I had.

EMPEROR: Mamillius, see that Phanocles does not lose by his visit. Mamillius!

MAMILLIUS: Caesar.

EMPEROR: And this lady? Is she your wife?

PHANOCLES: She is my sister.

EMPEROR: Your sister?

PHANOCLES: Euphrosyne, Caesar. A free woman and a virgin.

EMPEROR: Lady, let us see your face.

PHANOCLES: Caesar! She—

EMPEROR: You must accustom yourself to our western manners, Phanocles. We intend no discourtesy, lady. Modesty is the proper ornament of virginity. But let us see your face, so that we may know to whom we speak.

(EUPHROSYNE *with extreme reluctance lowers the veil.*)

Lady, you were well named for one of the Graces.

PHANOCLES: My sister!

MAMILLIUS: Phanocles, you bring us the tenth wonder of the world!

PHANOCLES: But Lord, I have not explained!

MAMILLIUS: "The speechless eloquence of beauty."

19

EMPEROR: I have heard that somewhere before. Has no sculptor seen your sister?

PHANOCLES: Sculptor?

MAMILLIUS: She should be immortalized as Aphrodite!

PHANOCLES: Daaah! Forgive me, Caesar—she is too modest—she is too sensitive—she—she—

EMPEROR: Calm yourself. No harm is intended to you or to your sister. Mamillius, they are our guests.

MAMILLIUS: Oh, yes, Grandfather!

PHANOCLES: My model—

EMPEROR: So you are a sculptor too?

MAMILLIUS: Phanocles and the lady Euphrosyne are the Emperor's guests!

(*During the ensuing speeches,* EUPHROSYNE *is removed in as much grave pomp as the company can muster.*)

PHANOCLES: My model!

MAMILLIUS: Take great care of her. Go with them, lady.

EMPEROR: Be happy, lady. You too, Phanocles.

MAMILLIUS: Farewell until a later hour!

EMPEROR: You speak verses. And now, Phanocles, come, sit down. A cup of wine to celebrate her—and your—arrival.

MAMILLIUS: A toast to beauty!

PHANOCLES: But my model! My working model!

EMPEROR: I divine your troubles, my dear Phanocles, and rest assured that they are all over. All, all, over. You shall have all the marble or bronze you want.

PHANOCLES: Marble is useless.

EMPEROR: Gold, perhaps.

MAMILLIUS: Warm, flesh-tinted alabaster.

EMPEROR: No, no. Pay no attention, Phanocles. Bronze. My dear boy, you are making me very happy! I rejoice with you.

MAMILLIUS: What is her voice like?

PHANOCLES: My sister's voice?

MAMILLIUS: How does she speak?

PHANOCLES: She speaks very seldom, Lord. I cannot

remember the quality of her voice.

MAMILLIUS: Men have built temples for objects of less beauty!

PHANOCLES: She is my sister!

EMPEROR: Have you promised her in marriage? Is she betrothed?

PHANOCLES: No, Caesar.

EMPEROR: But if you are so poor, Phanocles, has it never occurred to you that you might make a fortune by a brilliant connection?

PHANOCLES: (*blank*). What woman would you have me marry, Caesar?

MAMILLIUS: Has she an ambition?

EMPEROR: My dear Mamillius, a beautiful woman is her own ambition.

MAMILLIUS: She is all the reasons in the world for poetry!

PHANOCLES: (*angrily. Jumps up.*) I cannot follow you, Caesar. I cannot understand men. Of what importance is the bedding of individuals when there is such an ocean at our feet of eternal relationships to examine or confirm?

EMPEROR: Explain a little further.

PHANOCLES: If you let a stone drop from your hand it will fall.

EMPEROR: I hope we are following you.

PHANOCLES: Each substance has affinities of an eternal and immutable nature with every other substance. A man who understands them—this lord here—

EMPEROR: My grandson, the Lord Mamillius.

PHANOCLES: Lord, do you know much of law?

MAMILLIUS: It is my fate to be a Roman.

PHANOCLES: There then! You can move easily in the world of law. I can move easily in the world of substance and force because I credit the universe with at least a lawyer's intelligence. Just as you who know the law could have your way with me since I do not, so I can have my way with the universe.

EMPEROR: Confused, illogical, and extremely hubristic. Tell me, when you talk like this do people ever say you are mad?

21

PHANOCLES: Always, Caesar. That is why I severed my connection with the Library.

EMPEROR: I see. *Are* you a sculptor?

PHANOCLES: No. Am I mad?

EMPEROR: I think perhaps you are.

PHANOCLES: The universe is a mechanism.

MAMILLIUS: Are you a magician?

PHANOCLES: There is no magic.

MAMILLIUS: Your sister is the living proof and epitome of magic.

PHANOCLES: Then she is beyond Nature's legislation.

MAMILLIUS: That may well be. Is there any poetry in your universe?

PHANOCLES: That is how they all talk, Caesar—poetry, magic, religion—

EMPEROR: (*chuckling*). Be careful, Greek. You are talking to the High Pontiff of Jupiter.

PHANOCLES: Does Caesar believe in the things that the High Pontiff has to do?

EMPEROR: I prefer not to answer that question.

PHANOCLES: Lord Mamillius, do you believe in your very heart that there is an irrational and unpredictable force of poetry outside your rolls of paper?

MAMILLIUS: How dull your life must be!

PHANOCLES: Dull? My life is passed in a condition of ravished astonishment! Yet I am destitute. Without your help I must starve. With it I can change the universe.

EMPEROR: Are you a Christian?

PHANOCLES: Caesar—I swear—I am willing to sacrifice to you whenever you like—

EMPEROR: You believe in the gods then?

PHANOCLES: I—I am indifferent, Caesar, as I think you must be, together with all educated and thinking men.

EMPEROR: But you are not a Christian?

PHANOCLES: How should that contradictory mixture of hysterical beliefs appeal to such a man as I?

EMPEROR: Forgive me, Phanocles, but I like to be certain. I

am getting old and perhaps foolish. Executions distress me.

PHANOCLES: Executions?

EMPEROR: You were going to change the universe. Will you improve it?

MAMILLIUS: He is mad, Caesar.

EMPEROR: Phanocles, in my experience changes have seldom been for the better, since the universe does not seem to give something for nothing. Yet I entertain you for my—for your sister's sake. Be brief. What do you want?

PHANOCLES: With this ship you will be more famous than Alexander. Any one of the rich men I approached could have had that fame had they wanted it. Caesar!

EMPEROR: Ah, yes. Your ship. What is she called?

PHANOCLES: She has no name.

EMPEROR: A ship without a name? Find one, Mamillius.

MAMILLIUS: I do not care for her. Amphitrite, Grandfather, with your permission—

EMPEROR: I shall see you at dinner and further your education.

MAMILLIUS: I will ensure that our guest is comfortable.

EMPEROR: Do so. Mamillius!

MAMILLIUS: Grandfather—?

EMPEROR: I am sorry you are bored.

MAMILLIUS: Bored? I, bored? Yes, of course I am. Very, very, very.

(EXIT MAMILLIUS.)

EMPEROR: She is unseaworthy, flat-bottomed, with little sheer and bows like a corn barge. What are the ornaments? Have they a religious significance?

PHANOCLES: Hardly, Caesar.

EMPEROR: So after all you do want to play boats with me? If I were not charmed with your innocence I should be displeased at your presumption.

PHANOCLES: I have three toys for you, Caesar. This is only the first.

23

EMPEROR: Man, I have tried for the equivalent of at least three normal audiences to understand you. What do you want?

PHANOCLES: Have you ever seen water boiling in a pot?

EMPEROR: I have.

PHANOCLES: There is much steam evolved which escapes into the air. If the pot were closed, what would happen?

EMPEROR: The steam could not escape.

PHANOCLES: The pot would burst. The force exerted by steam is titanic.

EMPEROR: (*interested*) Really? Have you ever seen a pot burst?

PHANOCLES: Beyond Syria there is a savage tribe. They inhabit a land full of natural oil and inflammable vapour. When they desire to cook they lead the vapour through pipes into stoves at the sides of their houses. The meat these natives eat is tough and must be cooked for a long time. They put one heavy dish on top of another, inverted. Now the steam builds up a pressure under the pot that penetrates the meat and cooks it thoroughly and quickly.

EMPEROR: Will not the steam burst the pot?

PHANOCLES: There is the ingenuity of the device. If the pressure becomes too great it will lift the dish and allow the steam to escape. Steam could lift a weight that an elephant would baulk at.

EMPEROR: (*excited*). And the flavour, Phanocles! It will be confined with the steam! The whole wonderful intention of the comestible will be preserved by magic!

PHANOCLES: Now in a ship—Let me light this lamp inside the model.

EMPEROR: (*disregarding him*). I have always been a primitive where meat is concerned. To taste meat in its exquisite simplicity would be a return to those experiences of youth that time has blunted. There should be a wood fire, a healthy tiredness in the limbs, a robust red wine; and if possible, a sense of peril—(*pause*). Phanocles, we are on the verge of an immense discovery. What do the natives call their two dishes?

PHANOCLES: (*depressed*). A pressure cooker.

EMPEROR: How soon could you make me one? Or perhaps if we simply inverted one dish over another—Fish, do you think? Or fowl? I think on the whole one would detect the intensification most readily in fish.

PHANOCLES: Caesar!

EMPEROR: You must dine with me now and we will formulate a plan of action.

(THE EMPEROR *claps his hands.*

ENTER VALET.)

PHANOCLES: But my boat, Caesar!

(PAUSE)

EMPEROR: Amphitrite? I could give you anything you want, Phanocles. But come, let us dine.

PHANOCLES: When the wind fails, what happens to a ship?

(PAUSE—*then shrugs and signs to* VALET.)

EMPEROR: (*indulgently—he is now affable, seeing the value of* PHANOCLES). She waits for the next one. The master invokes a wind. Sacrifices and so on. Toga!

(VALET *starts the change of togas, rosewater, etc., with the help of another* SLAVE.)

PHANOCLES: But if he does not believe in a wind god?

EMPEROR: Then I suppose he does not get a wind.

PHANOCLES: But if the wind fails at a moment of crisis for your warships?

EMPEROR: The slaves row.

PHANOCLES: And when they tire?

EMPEROR: They are beaten.

PHANOCLES: But if they become so tired that beating is useless?

EMPEROR: Then they are thrown overboard. You have the Socratic method.

(PHANOCLES *groans.*)

You are tired and hungry. Have no fear for
yourself or your sister. You have both become
very precious to me and your sister shall be my
ward.

PHANOCLES: I do not think of her.

EMPEROR: (*puzzled*). What do you want, then?

PHANOCLES: I have tried to say. I want to build you a
warship after the pattern of Amphitrite.

EMPEROR: A warship is an expensive undertaking. I cannot
treat you as though you were a qualified ship-
wright when you are only a librarian.

PHANOCLES: Then give me a hull—any hull. Give me an old
corn barge if you will, and sufficient money to
convert her after this fashion.

EMPEROR: Of course, my dear Phanocles, anything you like.
I will give the necessary orders. Indeed, it will be
the second boat I have given away lately. Now,
let us dine.

PHANOCLES: And my other inventions?

EMPEROR: The pressure cooker?

PHANOCLES: No. What I have called an explosive.

EMPEROR: Something that claps out? How strange! What
would be the use of that? What is the third
invention?

PHANOCLES: I will keep it in reserve to surprise you.

EMPEROR: (*relieved*). Do so. Make your ship and your
clapper-outer and then surprise me with the third
invention. But first of all the pressure cooker. And
now let us dine.

PHANOCLES: Shall I bring the working model with me, Caesar?

EMPEROR: Amphitrite? No, no. On the whole, I think not.
Come, Phanocles.

PHANOCLES: I could explain the machinery—

EMPEROR: The circular contrivances?

PHANOCLES: I call them paddle-wheels—a mode of progression.
That globe in the centre is a boiler.

EMPEROR: A pressure cooker? A tiny little pressure—

PHANOCLES: Oh, no! Caesar! Please try to understand. There

26

is no *frivolity* here. My aim is to re-shape the whole future of humanity.

EMPEROR: Dear me. Then I had better give you an official position at once. Supposing I appoint you my Director-General of Experimental Studies— would that please you?

PHANOCLES: I? Caesar's Director-General? With leave to experiment?

EMPEROR: To your heart's content, my friend. But now we go to dine.

USHER: Caesar goes to dine!

(*Exit* EMPEROR.)

PHANOCLES: (*ecstatic, as he follows*) . . . with leave to experiment:

(EXIT PHANOCLES. *Trumpets off.* THE CAPTAIN *is released by the trumpets. He comes down stage, sheathing his sword as he does so. Pauses. Looks down funnel.* AMPHRITITE *starts to go—Peep! Peep! chuffa, chuffa, Poop! Poop!* CAPTAIN *leaps away. Draws his sword.*)

CAPTAIN: Sentry! Turn out the guard!

(CURTAIN)

ACT II

Scene: *Same as Act I.*

PHANOCLES *is discovered making calculations with the aid of a portable abacus which* EUPHROSYNE *is holding for him. He also has some sort of sighting instrument along which he squints out to sea from time to time and notes readings and results, etc., on tablets. All this intersperses the rather spasmodic phrasing of the opening speech.*

               (*Enter a* SEAMAN.)

SEAMAN: Director-General Phanocles, Sir.

PHANOCLES: What do you want?

SEAMAN: The Captain's compliments, Sir and beg to report that the magic ship is in all respects ready for sea.
(PHANOCLES NODS. EXIT SEAMAN.)

PHANOCLES: (*to* EUPHROSYNE). Is there anything more impenetrable than frivolity? How can I demonstrate the explosive here? Something that "claps out"! I tried to explain again. I was logical and precise; but he is like—I cannot tell what he is like;— what they are all like. Help me. In this mad race of men only you and I know true sanity; and yet sometimes you seem to know these people too. Would the young Lord Mamillius understand, do you think? Euphrosyne, make them understand the heat, the boundless force, the sudden expansion—(*Pause. She shakes her head*). Why must I waste my time on them? If I could only brush them aside—or show them my new heaven and new earth!
(ENTER CAPTAIN OF THE GUARD.)

CAPTAIN: Director-General—Phanocles!

PHANOCLES: What do you want?

CAPTAIN: There is a casket for you outside the door.

PHANOCLES: Ah, yes, yes. Why are they waiting? Let them bring it in at once. The Emperor may be here at any moment.

CAPTAIN: I can hardly do that, Phanocles. If the Emperor wants such a thing brought into the villa he is entitled to. That presents no difficulty. "Guard will reverse arms and assume an attitude of dejection" —and so on. But where are my instructions? Suppose this is not a dead body?

PHANOCLES: A body?

CAPTAIN: Imagine the black I should put up if I reversed arms and assumed an attitude of dejection while those men carried in a concealed assassin. Before the casket comes through that door the body must be examined, and in my presence.

(*The light dawns on* PHANOCLES.)

PHANOCLES: You want to open—

CAPTAIN: Of course I shall have every respect shown whilst confirming the melancholy truth.

PHANOCLES: Look if you must. But please hurry!

CAPTAIN: With your permission then.

PHANOCLES: Yes, yes—Captain!—On no account touch the butterfly.

(EXIT CAPTAIN.)

CAPTAIN: (*off*). Guard and men with arms—shun! Reverse arms!

PHANOCLES: Power in the hands of man. How shall I make him understand? Be merciful, Euphrosyne! What is a vow? You could be the link! You can choose for us—a new heaven and earth, or poverty again, and frustration.

(ENTER MAMILLIUS. *He stands contemplating* EUPHROSYNE.)

Lord Mamillius!—(*to* EUPHROSYNE). If only you would help me, Euphrosyne!

(PHANOCLES *approaches* MAMILLIUS.)

PHANOCLES : Lord Mamillius, what happens when lightning strikes a tree?

MAMILLIUS : If the tree is anywhere near the Imperial Precincts, my grandfather offers a sacrifice—How unbelievably ignorant you are, Phanocles! Surely you know that?

PHANOCLES : Euphrosyne! Explain to him—

MAMILLIUS : Yes—let your sister explain.

PHANOCLES : No, no—of course she must not. There was a vow . . .

MAMILLIUS : What does he mean, Euphrosyne?

PHANOCLES : Please let us be, Lord—(*He sees the* FOUR SLAVES). Ah!

(ENTER FOUR SLAVES *carrying an object which is as much like a coffin as the cast and the public will take.*)

Gently—carefully. . . . Round here. Lower that end. It must face this way.

(*He dismisses the slaves and examines the horrible box devoutly.*)

MAMILLIUS : How horrible! Lady, you should not be seen in company with so stark a reminder.

PHANOCLES : Lord, there is nothing to fear.

(PHANOCLES *removes the lid and reveals the black and yellow projectile standing on its stalk. It is the size of a man and more. It is very nasty.*)

MAMILLIUS : A new god!

PHANOCLES : Lord, this is my explosive. The whole mechanism is to be hurled from a catapult at what you wish to destroy. This will make your Empire irresistible.

MAMILLIUS : It is not my Empire!

PHANOCLES : Here is an arming vane. The pressure of the air makes it spin off—when this rod touches any solid object a compressive shock heats the explosive to the point where it catches fire. What happens then?

MAMILLIUS : Could your sister tell me?

PHANOCLES: The heat causes a sudden expansion. So what happens to the mechanism?

MAMILLIUS: It will become bigger.

PHANOCLES: No!

MAMILLIUS: Smaller?

PHANOCLES: No!

MAMILLIUS: Then, logically, Phanocles, it must remain the same size which is a pity. Any change would be for the better.

PHANOCLES: The mechanism changes—into vapour.

MAMILLIUS: You are a conjurer after all. Show me, sometime— but not now. I have a message for you. The Emperor is delayed by grave imperial business.

PHANOCLES: Delayed? You mean he's not coming? But my steamship! She is down there in the bay, waiting! He was to see her!

MAMILLIUS: No one could see much in this heat haze, Phanocles. We shall have thunder. Is your sister afraid of thunder?

PHANOCLES: This is—this was to be—one of the great days of the world—and he delays—he is signing— business—!

MAMILLIUS: Phanocles, I have just now remembered the second half of my grandfather's message. He wishes you to inspect the north wing of the villa; carefully; by yourself, Phanocles. He particularly wishes you to go by yourself.

PHANOCLES: What reason—?

MAMILLIUS: Reason?

PHANOCLES: But then—an Emperor does not always give a reason. . . .

MAMILLIUS: No, indeed. He need not necessarily find a reason.

PHANOCLES: What must I do there?

MAMILLIUS: Do? Just stay there, I suppose.

PHANOCLES: (*naughty temper*). He made me Director-General of Experimental Studies. Any architect, any builder, any hodman—

31

MAMILLIUS: He asks you—please—to calculate the number of
paving stones of different sizes in the corridors.
(PHANOCLES *registers what might be anything or
nothing!*)
(*sticking to it*)—and give him your comments if
you find any . . . any significant mathematical
relationships.

PHANOCLES: But my ship—my explosive—my sister—

MAMILLIUS: I will take care of them all. It is his Imperial Will,
Phanocles.

PHANOCLES: This is madness! I am lost, Lord. People defeat
me. (*Goes, muttering.*) Significant mathematical
relationships. . . . *All* mathematical relationships
are significant!

(EXIT PHANOCLES. MAMILLIUS *gives a gasp of relief,
looks furtively towards the* EMPEROR'S *apartments,
and then moves cautiously towards* EUPHROSYNE.)

MAMILLIUS: Are they, Lady? But not all human relationships. I have tried to follow you. Did you know
that? Did you? (*She nods.*) Have I annoyed you?
It would seem so. I cannot confuse this curious
and obsessive interest with the enchantment of the
blind god. Yet a glimpse of you walking the lawns
—even the knowledge as I pace the long corridors
that you are lying asleep behind this wall or this—
. . . I had a speech prepared, but now you stand
near me the words have flown out of my head.
This cannot be love; yet I cannot rest. I have
written poetry—Greek, of course—and some
whose judgement is of value think it good. But
your magic fits no verses. I have written and
erased till the wax melted. The ache, the frustration—my bewilderment—distil down from blown
verses through the single line to one cold drop of
truth—

"Euphrosyne is beautiful but dumb".
Silence and mystery are merciless weapons. Cease
to be the Egyptian Sphinx. Become a face, a voice

32

with accent, tricks of speech—with laughter and opinion; become an ordinary woman, and either conquer me outright for your empire, or set me free! No words? Must our meeting be this half-measure? (*Pause*) Oh, Lady, have mercy! I have tried to be honest—(*She looks at him suddenly.*)— a strange lower-middle-class word to hear spoken in an Emperor's villa! Your brother can change this mechanism into vapour. Could he change me too? I have it almost in my heart to wish he could! (*Goes to projectile.*)

EUPHROSYNE: No!

MAMILLIUS: You spoke! Euphrosyne—you spoke to me! You said "No!" What did I do?
(*He has left the box and gone to her.* EUPHROSYNE *has sunk back into silence, only shakes her head. After a second* MAMILLIUS *rushes back to the box.*)

EUPHROSYNE: (*starting up*). No!

MAMILLIUS: (*wreathed in delight*). Oh, but yes!
(*His hands fumble happily all over the explosive, keeping his eyes on* EUPHROSYNE. *She goes desperately over to between him and the box.*)

EUPHROSYNE: The butterfly—the brass butterfly! It is outside your world. You will kill us all!

MAMILLIUS: Is there a curse on it?

EUPHROSYNE: Yes—No. Look. This is a charm. He has stored the lightning in this metal egg. Have you ever worn a charm?

MAMILLIUS: All men wear them—to keep off the evil eye or fever.

EUPHROSYNE: As long as the charm sits there the lightning will not wake; but when my brother hurls the whole mechanism from a catapult the butterfly spins off. Then a touch would make lightning come from the egg, that would push this villa over and throw it into the sea.

MAMILLIUS: Only a touch?

EUPHROSYNE: Write your verses, Lord. Leave the lightning alone.

MAMILLIUS: You are . . . dawning on me.

EUPHROSYNE: You made me break a vow—

MAMILLIUS: You are so beautiful—

EUPHROSYNE: No more than you.

MAMILLIUS: How ignorant I was to think that hearing your voice would cure me of you! Euphrosyne! You said, "No more than you"! (*Pause*) I haunt you? We haunt each other. There is the honest truth. We are wonderful undiscovered country. Show me your face again.

EUPHROSYNE: I must go. Let me pass!

MAMILLIUS: I will see you—I must! Our haunting gives me the right to see you.

EUPHROSYNE: You are a prince.

MAMILLIUS: I? A prince? I am a poor bastard on a string! (*Pause*) And therefore what have I to lose? Show me your face. Come here. Closer. Your obedience is wonderful, and breaks my heart. Uncover your face.

(*She uncovers her face and they look at each other. She is dazzling.*)

I am lost. I am killed with kindness. Why would you not speak? Why did you hide this from me?

EUPHROSYNE: My vow.

MAMILLIUS: Euphrosyne, you are a person. You have been here and there. You have a history. There are things you like—

EUPHROSYNE: My voice and my face were to cure you.

MAMILLIUS: Do you begin to love me?

EUPHROSYNE: What good would it do to say yes?

MAMILLIUS: We shall spend our lives together.

EUPHROSYNE: No.

MAMILLIUS: My grandfather is the Emperor—

EUPHROSYNE: He would not give you a free woman against her will.

MAMILLIUS: Your vow? Let the Emperor absolve you.

EUPHROSYNE: No.

MAMILLIUS: You are your brother's ward. I can twist him

round my finger. Besides, he would never dare
to—

EUPHROSYNE: (*defiantly*) Do not speak like that! My brother is
a great man. His name will outlast Caesar's!

MAMILLIUS: A conjuror! A toy-maker!

EUPHROSYNE: What are you, with your verses, to speak of him?
He says, "Let such and such a new thing be"—as
though he were—He could throw a chain round
the stars!

MAMILLIUS: I could throw a rope round his neck! May he
count cobbles till his eyes cross!

EUPHROSYNE: (*suddenly frightened*). Go away. Let me alone. I
will have nothing to do with you. You are cruel,
like all the rest; you want to harm and humiliate
—perhaps to murder him. We might be from
another kind of earth, I and my brother . . . your
conjurer! He is ignorant in some ways—but you!
(*She bursts into tears.*)

MAMILLIUS: Euphrosyne—forgive me! I didn't think what I was
saying, nor how it would hurt you—I meant what
I said as a joke, Euphrosyne—as a *joke*! I was only
joking!
(*Pause*)

EUPHROSYNE: Oh . . .

MAMILLIUS: Are we friends again?

EUPHROSYNE: I want to be—more than anything, since the vow
is broken. But we are so different. Somehow I have
never been able to laugh at jokes the way other
people do. I don't think I have a sense of humour.

MAMILLIUS: I love you as you are, so—
(*Enter* EMPEROR.)
—adorably grave, even when you are happy, and
you *are* happy now, aren't you? Please, please say
you are happy!

EMPEROR: Well, Mamillius, I have news for you. Euphrosyne
—(*she sniffs*) Crying? What a bully!

MAMILLIUS: I did nothing!

EMPEROR: I was not referring to you, Mamillius.

35

MAMILLIUS: Tell me the secret of success in love.

EMPEROR: Decision. It is irresistible. Dear me. . . . Judging by the almost hysterical ugliness of the figure and the mortal overtones of the box, I must assume this to be one of the inventions of my Director-General.

MAMILLIUS: The figure turns into vapour.

(ENTER PHANOCLES.)

PHANOCLES: Caesar! At a rough computation, the tiles in the north wing number eleven thousand. I could not count them exactly.

(THE EMPEROR *awaits further enlightenment.*)

However, Caesar, this is a great day in the history of the world. When projected from the catapult which I have placed down there on the quay, the brass arming vane flies off. Then, in contact with a solid object—

EMPEROR: —Flies off. That reminds me, Phanocles—the demonstration is cancelled.

PHANOCLES: (*an outburst*). Cancelled? My demonstration? What business—what right—I come to the top— I climb from nowhere with this head and these hands—I come to the peak among men, and you are like the others! Where shall I find someone who can understand? In this—this ant-hill of blind and indifferent humanity—among these wars and—and catastrophes. . . . Last night there was an eclipse of the moon. I could not see it, but the slave described it to me—the still movement, that fated advance of the copper shadow. . . . Oh, the majestic distances! They are real. We grow up into them. They are man's true empire of the mind—and of the body. . . . But only I of all men —I alone—I by myself—I have no brother—the ants—there is nothing. Nothing. No one. . . .

(*During this speech the* EMPEROR *takes more and more care to be imperial. He does it, perhaps, by being rather than by doing.*

36

EUPHROSYNE *holds* PHANOCLES, *pulling him back,
both hands on his left arm. She is turned, petrified,
towards the* EMPEROR.
The enormity of the occasion has dawned on
MAMILLIUS, *who is acutely conscious that* PHANOCLES'
*raw knees are on his account. He sees the change in
grandfather long before* PHANOCLES *sees it.*)

EMPEROR: Mamillius.

MAMILLIUS: Caesar?

EMPEROR: There is news from Tripoli.

MAMILLIUS: From Postumus?

EMPEROR: He has broken off his campaign. He has concen-
trated his army on the seaport and he is stripping the
coast of ships, from fishing-boats to triremes.

MAMILLIUS: He is tired of heroics.

EMPEROR: No, Mamillius. He is a realist, and realists are
always frightened.

MAMILLIUS: Postumus? Frightened?

EMPEROR: He fears your influence.

MAMILLIUS: Postumus—frightened of me?

EMPEROR: You are too intelligent not to know why; and too
inexperienced to appreciate our danger.

MAMILLIUS: But he thinks me an incompetent fool!

EMPEROR: He is right, of course. But he knows also that
incompetence and folly have not prevented a
number of my predecessors from attaining to this
purple. And he has heard—I think—that the
Emperor's affectionately regarded grandson is
taking an interest in ships and weapons of war.

MAMILLIUS: What shall we do?

EMPEROR: I shall go to Tripoli to convince him that I am
still Emperor and that you do not want to be the
next one.

MAMILLIUS: But that will be dangerous!

EMPEROR: My dear Mamillius, have you begun to think of
other people? Where will this end?

MAMILLIUS: I shall come with you.

EMPEROR: Bless you, child!—do you want your throat cut?

37

MAMILLIUS: My throat?

EMPEROR: I do not think that Postumus would accord you the privilege of committing suicide.

MAMILLIUS: I am a man.

EMPEROR: Officially.

MAMILLIUS: And therefore I shall come with you to Tripoli. When do we leave?

EMPEROR: As soon as this heat haze lifts. Towards evening. I—we must get there before Postumus leaves. When Postumus moves, he does so with frightening speed. He was here, on his last welcome visit, two days before I expected him.

MAMILLIUS: I shall *play* the man.

EMPEROR: What a curious turn of phrase! But apt. Something has happened to you, and I am delighted. But be careful, Mamillius. We are dealing with a superb man of action.

MAMILLIUS: I shall surprise you.

EMPEROR: You have done that already. (*As if noticing him for the first time.*) Ah, Director-General, here you are at last. The very man I wanted for advice and information.

MAMILLIUS: I shall make my preparations now. Phanocles, take great care of Euphrosyne.

EMPEROR: Make your preparations?

MAMILLIUS: We are going to the army.

(EXIT MAMILLIUS.)

EMPEROR: What did he mean by that? Have you noticed, Phanocles, that today the normal means of human communication have seemed to be a little inadequate?

PHANOCLES: I have noticed it all my life, Caesar.

EMPEROR: You are a philosopher. What a pity to cancel the demonstration! Now I shall have to try your pressure cooker on my return.

PHANOCLES: My pressure cooker?

EMPEROR: Had you forgotten that we were to dine together this evening and try your pressure cooker?

Politics, administration, dynastic emergencies. . . .
Never consent to be an Emperor, Phanocles. To
be the servant of all men is a worthy ideal, no
doubt, but restless, restless. . . . How *fast* will your
steamship take us to Tripoli?

PHANOCLES: My—?

EMPEROR: Amphitrite.

PHANOCLES: My steamship!

EMPEROR: She is ready, of course.

(PHANOCLES *makes an inarticulate noise*.)

You must go aboard her now, Phanocles, and
prepare her for the voyage. Tripoli is hardly a
majestic distance, but it is far enough.

PHANOCLES: She will take you there twice as fast as your
fastest ship, Caesar! Oh . . . Caesar!

EMPEROR: I have an irrational faith in you, Director-
General. That is unwise, of course.
Go now. But let your sister stay here for a
moment. Oh—and Phanocles—

PHANOCLES: Caesar?

EMPEROR: Remove this object, will you?

PHANOCLES: My explosive?

EMPEROR: Or vaporize it, if you prefer. Could you do that
quickly?

PHANOCLES: (*laughing*). I should knock the villa down, Caesar.
Let me have it loaded on the catapult down by
the quay. Then, perhaps, when you are leaving in
Amphitrite—

EMPEROR: Do so.

PHANOCLES: You men—take it back to the quay!

(ENTER THE FOUR SLAVES. *They box up the projectile
and go out towards the quay during the following
speeches*.)

EMPEROR: Twice as fast?

PHANOCLES: At least, Caesar.

EMPEROR: I must confess to a perhaps childish delight in the
thought of approaching Postumus, of all people,
with terrifying speed. Our steamship will take the

	wind out of his sails, Phanocles.
PHANOCLES:	Yes, Caesar. I shall go now, Caesar. (*Pauses at door.*) Caesar—how far is it to Tripoli?
EMPEROR:	About three days' sail at this season. In winter, of course, it is either much further—as much as eight days—or disastrously nearer.
PHANOCLES:	Pardon, Caesar . . . miles?
EMPEROR:	Well?
PHANOCLES:	To Tripoli, Caesar.
EMPEROR:	Miles to Tripoli? You are a baffling mixture of genius and ignorance. Surely you know we cannot reach Tripoli by land?
PHANOCLES:	There must be a fixed distance.
EMPEROR:	I fail to see why we should interest ourselves in such an academic consideration at this juncture. Tell your captain to be ready to leave when the haze lifts. You *have* a captain?
PHANOCLES:	Yes, Caesar.
EMPEROR:	You chose him carefully?
PHANOCLES:	Yes, Caesar.
EMPEROR:	A lucky and religious man?
PHANOCLES:	I don't know.
EMPEROR:	To what an enterprise am I committing myself! On land, Phanocles, although I am the All Father's High Pontiff, I should be the first to admit that the workings of his divine nature are often inexplicably random and obscure; but once surrounded by water. . . . We must take ample provisions, for frequent sacrifices will be necessary.
PHANOCLES:	(*going*). We shall get there twice as fast as your ships can move, Caesar.
	(EXIT PHANOCLES. EMPEROR *goes to* EUPHROSYNE.)
EMPEROR:	Still frightened and silent after all these weeks, Euphrosyne? Come! Are you not yet accustomed to our unpretentious little retreat? In Rome, now —ha, Rome! There you might well be over-awed, child. Rome is a really intimidating symbol of the Imperial Power.

(USHER ENTERS *right*; *crosses left, and signs with his finger*.)

SENTRY: (*off*). Guard—turn out!

EMPEROR: But here, at peace, and with the minimum of ceremonial—
(USHER EXITS *right*.)
—where I am no more than any other country gentleman, surely you can accept us as the kindly and unaffected folk we are?

OFFICER: (*off*). Left-right left-right left-right—halt! Into line—right turn! Pick up your dressing.

EMPEROR: Forgive this insistence, Euphrosyne; but the happiness of that golden youth, my grandson, is very near to me. What is your mystery?

EUPHROSYNE: I cannot tell you.

EMPEROR: Shall I guess then? This remarkable man who passes as your brother—are you not in fact his wife?

EUPHROSYNE: No.

EMPEROR: What are you hiding? Look at me. (*Pause*) Child, you are frightened of me. That is terrible. Can you not understand what a humiliation that is? I learn now, and for the first time, that the young and charming, the poor and the helpless, see not the man, but the position. They do not see me as the ultimate guardian of justice—and perhaps even mercy. They hear only the fanfares, they are blinded by the purple and the gold. I beg you, child—for his sake, but also for mine—see what infinite power lies in the soft cheek of a girl! Do not humiliate me.

EUPHROSYNE: Forgive me, Caesar. I want to tell you—but I have not found the courage. We have lived for so long in fear, my brother and I; here at least we have achieved a sort of peace in your kindness . . . but strange new things have happened—miracles you could call them—

41

EMPEROR: What miracles? Do you mean your brother's in-
genious toys?

EUPHROSYNE: Oh no, Caesar. My brother is a great man, but
still only a man. . . .

EMPEROR: Go on.

EUPHROSYNE: I dare not.

EMPEROR: But why?

EUPHROSYNE: Because you *are* Caesar.

EMPEROR: So I am useless, although they have made me
Father of the Country and High Priest of all the
gods? And after all, officially I am a god myself.

EUPHROSYNE: (*in terror*). Be merciful! Let me go now—please,
Caesar!

(PAUSE)

EMPEROR: Oh. I see. Or perhaps I think I see.

EUPHROSYNE: (*almost inaudible*). Yes, Caesar.

(PAUSE)

EMPEROR: Now, what were we talking about? Strange how
completely a recent conversation, with all its
implications, can vanish out of mind! As I was
saying, my dear Euphrosyne, you will grow accus-
tomed to our little retreat. You may go now, and
return when we are leaving in order to bid us
farewell. You will hear the Captain of the Guard,
even in the women's quarters. He is a very good
soldier.

(EXIT EUPHROSYNE. THE EMPEROR *busies himself
with documents. Bustle. Passing of slaves with
baggage.* USHER, *among them, announces*
MAMILLIUS, *since he sees him off and is transfixed.*)

USHER: Caesar—the Lord Mamillius.

(EXIT USHER. ENTER MAMILLIUS. *He is dressed in what
he conceives to be a truly martial costume. Starting at
the ground floor: the soles of his shoes are three inches
thick. He got this from Greek tragic acting and it is
a good idea if you are used to it.* MAMILLIUS *is not,
so that when he moves it feels as though he is lifting
pieces of pavement with him. The red and blue*

42

*leather of the boots comes to just below his knees,
but is hidden in front by brass greaves that flare
over each knee into knobs and spikes. These are
effective and decorative when kept apart by a horse,
but* MAMILLIUS *dislikes horses, and in any case has
not got one with him. He takes care, therefore, to
leave a gap between them since, if he does not, they
catch and release with a sudden melodious twang. It
is fortunate that spurs have not been invented. Above
the greaves is a short skirt of red and blue stripes,
partly hidden by brass scale armour, and topped by a
belt from which hangs a long sword—much longer
than a Roman one. Above the belt again is a brass
cuirass, heavily decorated. In the middle of all these
decorations is a Gorgon's head whose expression is
partly due to her deadly nature and partly to sheer
astonishment at finding herself where she is. The
arms are covered with scale armour, and the right one
is holding against the hip a helmet big enough for a
diver.* MAMILLIUS *knows the Bacchae of Euripides by
heart and this helmet has three crests instead of one
—each with plumes on.* MAMILLIUS *advances as
casually as his costume will allow him. If he were
not intensely civilized he would probably whistle.
His red and blue striped cloak reaches to where his
spurs would be if he had them.
It is some time before the* EMPEROR *believes his eyes.*
MAMILLIUS *tries meanwhile to convince himself that
his recent and haunting suspicion of his own foolish-
ness is nonsense.*)

MAMILLIUS: Well, Grandfather, I have made my preparations.
  EMPEROR: (*Pause.*) Did no one point out the significance of
           the colour to you?
MAMILLIUS: Colour, Grandfather?
  EMPEROR: That near imperial purple.
MAMILLIUS: Oh, but I was particularly careful, Grandfather.
           There is not a touch of purple in the whole
           costume. Just red and blue stripes.

EMPEROR: That was very delicate of you, Mamillius. How many people have seen this . . . this regalia?

MAMILLIUS: Only the craftsmen, Grandfather. I designed the whole thing myself. I wanted to surprise you.

EMPEROR: You have.

MAMILLIUS: (*gaining a little confidence*). As a matter of fact, I've kept it by me for some time.

EMPEROR: I suppose that thing is a helmet?

MAMILLIUS: (*losing it all*). Thing? You don't really like—

EMPEROR: Put it on.

MAMILLIUS: This?

EMPEROR: That.

MAMILLIUS: Oh no, Grandfather. It gives me a headache.

EMPEROR: You have worn it? Often?

MAMILLIUS: Only in private, Grandfather—perhaps, after all, for a sea voyage this isn't—

EMPEROR: Put it on!

(MAMILLIUS *puts on the helmet.* THE EMPEROR *loses all but a shred of self-control. He laughs silently for what seems to* MAMILLIUS *to be about an hour. He shrinks into his armour and looks, if possible, even sillier. This finishes the* EMPEROR, *who collapses in cackles.*)

MAMILLIUS: You are treating me as a child! I grant you that the costume is unfortunate; but there is a man inside!

(*This last remark, taken in conjunction with* MAMILLIUS'S *almost total disappearance between cuirass and helmet, sets the* EMPEROR *off again.*)

Am I so funny?

(*A curious thing happens.* MAMILLIUS *begins to grin, to giggle and then to laugh. As he does this he begins to emerge.*)

It was all right in private, Grandfather—but an audience—!

(*They are laughing side by side.*)

EMPEROR: Can you sit down?

MAMILLIUS: I've never tried.

44

EMPEROR: Try now.

MAMILLIUS: What a fool was I! There! Achilles can bend in the middle.

EMPEROR: If only Postumus could see you!

MAMILLIUS: I should not care for Postumus to laugh at me.

EMPEROR: He is humourless. Do you know, Mamillius, something has come to me. That wonderful costume of yours is the real reason for his return.

MAMILLIUS: But no one knew!

EMPEROR: My dear man! His agent sleeps under your pillow.

MAMILLIUS: You never told me.

EMPEROR: I have an old-fashioned belief in the protective powers of innocence. But that applies no longer.

MAMILLIUS: Should I stand up?

EMPEROR: Do not risk more movements than are necessary.

MAMILLIUS: (*takes off his helmet and puts it in his lap*). I must go back and remove all the metal and put it with my hoop and my shuttlecock. And perhaps with my poems.

EMPEROR: You must give me the poems to keep.

MAMILLIUS: So I shall—all but one. What have I to hide from a man who has seen me in this? I wonder if that haze is lifting?
(*He goes clumsily to centre and looks through the door.*)

EMPEROR: You must make a special dedication of the helmet.

MAMILLIUS: To Mars himself! (*Puts the helmet on bust.*)

EMPEROR: Be careful!

MAMILLIUS: How wonderful he looks! General Postumus— shun! Slo-o-ope arms!

CAPTAIN: (*off*). Guard and men with arms—shun!

EMPEROR: You see, Mamillius? You have touched off some automatic response in the military mind.

MAMILLIUS: Guard and men with arms—

EMPEROR: No, no. You must not make fun of them.

MAMILLIUS: Present arms!

CAPTAIN: (*off*). Guard and men with arms—present arms!

(ENTER POSTUMUS. LONGISH SILENCE.)

EMPEROR: (*recovering*). Welcome home, Postumus! You have saved us the trouble of coming to see you.

MAMILLIUS: Hullo, Postumus.

POSTUMUS: Mamillius in arms.

MAMILLIUS: For show only, Postumus. I do not want to be an . Emperor.

POSTUMUS: You are not going to be. Captain, dismiss the Guard.

CAPTAIN: (*off*). Sir! Guard! Order arms. Turning right— dismiss!

POSTUMUS: Where are the rest of your men?

EMPEROR: There may be one or two in the gardens, Postumus. Why do you ask?

(ENTER USHER.)

USHER: General. . . .

POSTUMUS: See that the life of the villa beyond this room is normal.

EMPEROR: Yes. Do that, Chamberlain. (EXIT USHER.) What else can we do to make you feel at home? I deduce, Postumus, from your behaviour, that something has been worrying you. Let us be frank. What is it?

POSTUMUS: Listen. (*Reads*) "Ships and weapons of war are being built or converted and conveyed to the island of Capri for the Emperor's inspection. He and the Lord Mamillius are experimenting with large-scale methods of poisoning food."

EMPEROR: I suppose that refers to the pressure cooker.

MAMILLIUS: You bribed someone to spy on the Emperor!

EMPEROR: No, no, Mamillius. A man with prospects as brilliant as the Heir Designate does not need to pay cash for anything.

POSTUMUS: "The Lord Mamillius is in a state of high excite- ment—"

MAMILLIUS: Postumus—I swear—

POSTUMUS: Look at yourself!

(ENTER PHANOCLES.)

46

PHANOCLES: Caesar! They would not let me go on the quay—
EMPEROR: Who would not?
PHANOCLES: Soldiers.
POSTUMUS: Where were you going?
PHANOCLES: To my steamship.
POSTUMUS: So you are Phanocles. Stay where you are! Caesar, you may have an explanation that will satisfy me —I see now that no one could take this boy and his armour seriously—but there are too many strange things going on. In the circumstances, as Heir Designate, I felt it my duty to return. You are growing too old for responsibility, Caesar. We must establish a regency. *I* shall be Regent.
MAMILLIUS: But Postumus! You cannot really suppose that Caesar would be so foolish as to alter the succession for my sake!
POSTUMUS: You may think not. But he would bridge the Adriatic to please you.
MAMILLIUS: And you call yourself a realist!
POSTUMUS: I take no chances, even with fools, Mamillius. They may be fools who are very lucky. Know yourself, then. You are an old man's folly.
EMPEROR: You have never wanted my affection, Postumus, so you have never missed it. If I have been foolish enough to think that I could enjoy his company without more than the usual scandal, I have been wise enough to know that you are the best man to rule the Empire—however uncongenial I may find you personally.
MAMILLIUS: Let the Greek explain what has been done.
PHANOCLES: Lord—I am altering the whole circumstance of life. . . .
EMPEROR: He has this curious manner of speech, Postumus.
PHANOCLES: My ship, Lord—that was not intended to do you any harm. I am joining the ends of the world together. There will be no slaves, but coal and iron.
POSTUMUS: And men will fly!

47

PHANOCLES: Of course. Think of the problem of communication, Lord. You are a soldier. What is your greatest difficulty?

POSTUMUS: (*fiercely*). I have no difficulty!

PHANOCLES: But if you had?

POSTUMUS: Getting there first.

PHANOCLES: You see, Lord? It has been the same for every soldier. Communications.

EMPEROR: (*agreeably*). Yes, indeed. They should be made as difficult as possible.

PHANOCLES: My ship would set men free! My ship will—

POSTUMUS: You have no ship. I gave orders for them to burn her.

PHANOCLES: Burn my steamship! You burnt her!—Oh, Caesar!

POSTUMUS: I don't know what your game was, Caesar, but, as I said, I take no chances.

PHANOCLES: All that work . . . all that thought. . . .

MAMILLIUS: You still have your explosive, Phanocles.

POSTUMUS: Explosive?

EMPEROR: He has loaded some new projectile on the catapult down by the quay.

POSTUMUS: I saw the thing. What is it?

MAMILLIUS: He turns it into vapour. Explain, Phanocles.

PHANOCLES: My ship. . . .

EMPEROR: Yes. Explain, Phanocles, to please me. We must be quite clear about your inventions, Phanocles. They have troubled the Heir Designate. His projectile digs a hole, Postumus—some kind of spade. Useful!

PHANOCLES: How can I explain, Caesar? You are all like children!

EMPEROR: Speak to us as children, then.

PHANOCLES: Big egg falls on ground and goes—boom! Flames and smoke, and big, big hole! Earthquake! Volcano! Enemy men run away. . . . I can't do it, Caesar! To speak so to grown men—

EMPEROR: I said speak to us as children—not as babes in

48

arms. . . . You must make allowances, Postumus.

POSTUMUS: This big hole—could you make it in a city wall?

PHANOCLES: You burnt my ship!

POSTUMUS: If you treat me with disrespect I shall have you burnt yourself. Could you make the big hole in this villa?

PHANOCLES: I could destroy the whole villa.

POSTUMUS: An army too?

PHANOCLES: If I made the explosive large enough.

EMPEROR: Phanocles, what on earth are you saying? It is important that you be serious and truthful.

POSTUMUS: And that was the weapon you had trained seaward, ready for my ships!

PHANOCLES: I was aiming the catapult at a rock.

POSTUMUS: You see? Lies everywhere! But we'll soon know the truth. You, Greek, come with n... And I'll take the boy too, Caesar—just as a precaution.

EMPEROR: I forbid him to go with you, and I beg you to think carefully what you do, Postumus. For the last time, no one is trying to deceive you! These things are what they appear—harmless laboursaving devices—

(COMMOTION OFF)

SERGEANT: (*off*). General . . . General Postumus—

POSTUMUS: What was that? Who's there?

SERGEANT: (*off*). Sir! Sir!

POSTUMUS: (*draws sword*). All of you stay where you are. Here I am, man.

(ENTER BLEEDING SERGEANT.)

SERGEANT: The men, sir! Something horrible, sir!

POSTUMUS: Who sent you? Who is your officer?

SERGEANT: The officer's dead, sir. Drowned.

POSTUMUS: Make your report, Sergeant.

SERGEANT: We were in the other ship, sir—not yours.

EMPEROR: *Other* ship?

SERGEANT: Yes, Caesar. Our two were in advance of the Fleet. We got orders to burn the magic ship, so we went alongside—

POSTUMUS: Make your report to *me*, Sergeant!

SERGEANT: The boarding was dead easy, sir. The Captain shouts "Oars!" and out went the oars, straight and firm and level as a road. We got the word —"Away, boarders!" and we all charges out along the oars and on to the magic ship. There was hardly any crew to speak of for a ship that size, and what there was we knocks on the head with no trouble at all. . . .

PHANOCLES: I trained these men . . . there are no more like them!

POSTUMUS: Come to the point quickly! What happened to my men?

SERGEANT: Well, sir, we set her on fire, sir, like you said— and she burnt like a volcano!

PHANOCLES: Then you sank her?

SERGEANT: Yes, sir—but not before she woke up and went mad. She was alive, sir—I swear it! The few that escaped and are able to talk will bear me out. When the flames got hold, sir, they made her big brass belly scream at us, and those wooden wheels went round. She moved, sir—I swear she did—of her own—moved through the water without rowers or the wind! Those wheels caught us, sir, and we was set on fire, and then she swung round faster and faster and chewed up your own ship, just like as if she was a giant shark, sir! The sea was all full of men drowning and burning and screaming, and she was screaming and I was screaming—we were all screaming—

POSTUMUS: (*the fighting leader*). Company Sergeant Pyrrhus, Leading Sergeant of A Company in the invincible Roman Army of General Postumus—*SHUN!* (THE SERGEANT "*shuns*" *and holds it for some seconds.*) That's better! Now stand easy and tell me how many escaped.

SERGEANT: (*quietly*). Not much more than a dozen, sir—

fighting fit, that is . . . they were burnt a bit, most of 'em—I'm senior.

POSTUMUS: (*grimly*). I see. I'm glad you're safe, Sergeant. (*Turning to* PHANOCLES.) So you were altering the circumstance of life, were you? And you altered it at the cost of nearly two hundred of my men. I shall let their comrades try you. They will know best how to alter what is left of *your* life. (*He turns to the* EMPEROR.) And you, Caesar, plotted nothing with this Greek monstrosity—or with this little fancy bastard! Of course not! You just wanted to see how fierce your little pet could look in such pretty armour—and with purple frills too!

EMPEROR: Postumus, a thought has just occured to me. I am beginning to understand. You have been—how shall I put it?—

MAMILLIUS: —bluffing.

(EUPHROSYNE *appears in the doorway, unseen, and stands listening.*)

EMPEROR: We heard no drums. You are separated from your Fleet. You had only two ships, and now they are sunk.

MAMILLIUS: You've been hurrying on, Postumus—getting there first—moving with terrified speed—

POSTUMUS: What if I have? The Fleet will be here in a few hours, and I've men enough to hold the quay and you haven't even a guard!—ships that go mad—armour—explosives—whatever they might be! Sergeant!

SERGEANT: Sir?

POSTUMUS: Could you aim that catapult?

SERGEANT: I done fifteen years with the Mark Seven, sir.

POSTUMUS: Train it round away from the sea. Aim it inland. Aim it at this villa, for that matter—

SERGEANT: Sir—

(EUPHROSYNE *who has crept up stage, now silently darts off.*)

Do I loose it, sir?

POSTUMUS: A big hole, you said, Phanocles? Flames and smoke?

PHANOCLES: This is a nightmare. . . .

POSTUMUS: No. Let's just train it round, Sergeant. If we fire it we shall wait till the Fleet arrives. We shall let all the troops share in the fun.

SERGEANT: Sir.

POSTUMUS: Meanwhile, stand guard within earshot and keep your sword drawn.

SERGEANT: Yes, sir.

(EXIT SERGEANT. POSTUMUS *calms down, since he has now the whip hand again.*)

POSTUMUS: You know me, Caesar.

EMPEROR: Indeed, I thought so.

MAMILLIUS: I know him, Grandfather. He's frightened.

POSTUMUS: I? Frightened? There is reason for you to be frightened, Mamillius. I am arresting you.

MAMILLIUS: Try.

POSTUMUS: Do you think you can fight me?

EMPEROR: Postumus—Phanocles was right. This is a nightmare. Neither I nor the boy wish any harm to you. You are Heir Designate. What more do you want?

POSTUMUS: You had better both prepare to sail with me to Rome. As for the boy—he is under arrest. Give me your sword.

(MAMILLIUS *draws his sword.*)

MAMILLIUS: Come and take it.

EMPEROR: Postumus! This is open rebellion!

POSTUMUS: Is it possible that he *wants* me to run him through? If you are sensible, Caesar, the whole thing can be disposed of with the minimum of fuss.

EMPEROR: What is your proposal?

POSTUMUS: Consent to the arrest of this boy.

EMPEROR: And then?

POSTUMUS: Then you may remain in your villa and I shall go to Rome with your signed appointment of me as

Regent—or co-ruler, if you prefer the old forms.

EMPEROR: And then?

POSTUMUS: What then?

EMPEROR: The boy.

POSTUMUS: Surely you must realize, Caesar—

EMPEROR: —that he would die quickly—or perhaps slowly....

POSTUMUS: Before that, he would have a fair and unbiased trial.

EMPEROR: What do you think of my health?

POSTUMUS: Good, for your age.

EMPEROR: What would you think of it after I signed such a document?

POSTUMUS: Frankly I should cease to think of it.

EMPEROR: The care of my health would doubtless be given to others. I should have, perhaps, a month to live.

POSTUMUS: I am a ruler, and a Roman. Greek, come down to the quay with me.

MAMILLIUS: No, Phanocles—get behind me.

POSTUMUS: Why, Mamillius! Both I and my agent under-estimated you. So much the worse for you.

MAMILLIUS: I intend to live as long as I can.

POSTUMUS: Look out there, Mamillius. What do you see?

MAMILLIUS: Water.

POSTUMUS: Look at the horizon.

MAMILLIUS: Ships.

POSTUMUS: My ships, Mamillius. Nine thousand men.

MAMILLIUS: Coward!

POSTUMUS: For making certain? Enjoy yourself. When the men land I shall sweep this island in form and force. You have rather less than two hours to live.

EMPEROR: Let us come to some composition.

POSTUMUS: Before he drew his little sword we might have done so. But why should I argue now? My ships do that for me.

(EXIT POSTUMUS.)

MAMILLIUS: What shall we do?

EMPEROR: Phanocles could not arrange for our sudden transportation through the air to Rome?

PHANOCLES: No, Caesar.

EMPEROR: Then we must eat and drink and be quietly merry.

MAMILLIUS: I could not eat.

EMPEROR: I think with such clarity when eating. Something may yet be done. Mamillius, Phanocles and—and perhaps the girl. Or no. Better not the girl. I am thinking of her safety, Mamillius. No harm will come to her if she stays in the women's quarters. Phanocles, Director-General of Experimental Studies, the cancelled demonstration is re-decreed. We shall try your pressure cooker!

(*He beats the gong.*)

(CURTAIN)

ACT III

Scene: *The same.*

PHANOCLES, *detached and brooding.* MAMILLIUS, *at the wall, looking towards the quay.*

MAMILLIUS: He has lifted the weapon towards us like a malicious finger. I can see his ships in dozens crawling down from the horizon. When the wind shifts you can hear them. Can your ideas turn them back? (*No answer from* PHANOCLES.) At least Euphrosyne is safe. If I were noble and brave, that ought to be a comfort to me. Help me to die! Instead, it makes me sick. She is my happiness, and if I were sure of immortality I'd want to take her with me—to die also. D'you hear that, Phanocles? I tell myself I love your sister, yet here I am wanting her to die. (*Pause*) Ah, but suppose she insisted on dying with me! How beautiful! Then of course I couldn't possibly allow it. . . . Could I, Phanocles? I must say, for a Greek you are astonishingly taciturn.

PHANOCLES: What did I do to get myself here?

MAMILLIUS: You wrote a petition. Try it on Postumus.

PHANOCLES: A petition. A reasonable statement from one man to another. I have asked from men nothing but good will and commonsense. Yet the Emperor of the world is preoccupied in there, eating from a toy I would never have thought worth making. And down there a fool's finger is on my own trigger. We build on the expectation of man's goodness and the foundations collapse under us. We reveal to him the movement of the stars, the reasonable miracles of creation—and he buries

55

his nose in filth like a dog!

MAMILLIUS: You are so great and so clever, Phanocles—

PHANOCLES: I am a fool!

MAMILLIUS: All this cosmic intelligence. . . . Can you keep back those ships?

PHANOCLES: (*kindly*). No.

MAMILLIUS: No! Because there is a truly great man facing us on the quay—a great ruler—a great general. . . . Presently he will prove that greatness for all time and in the established manner by cutting our throats!

PHANOCLES: Yes.

MAMILLIUS: And you can do nothing?

PHANOCLES: No. The island is his. I can reveal miracles, Lord; I cannot perform them.

MAMILLIUS: The sword is mightier than the pen?

PHANOCLES: Yes, Lord.

MAMILLIUS: Think, man! What hope have we but you?

PHANOCLES: The Emperor, perhaps?

MAMILLIUS: You know he thinks of nothing but the pressure cooker! "While there is still time," he said. He said, "This may be the fine flower of a life's experience." Phanocles, I am devoted to the arts, but that is gastronomy to excess!

PHANOCLES: Help yourself, Lord. I cannot help you.

MAMILLIUS: We're going to change the universe!

PHANOCLES: I am incapable.

MAMILLIUS: How? Come here. Suppose you were the Heir Designate—put yourself in his place. He suspects me unjustly . . . well, perhaps I *have* had foolish thoughts of what it would be like to be Emperor, but not, not—

PHANOCLES: Not to excess?

MAMILLIUS: Exactly. (*Pause*) If we can understand him perhaps we can defeat him. Think, man. You are he. You look up at the villa. You think: "The old man is getting senile. The Greek is a magician. The boy is completely helpless by himself." Now,

56

Phanocles, what would you do next?

PHANOCLES: If I were Postumus?

MAMILLIUS: Yes. (*Pause*)

PHANOCLES: I should wish I were Phanocles! (*Proudly*)
(ENTER THE EMPEROR *in a high state of excitement and emotion.*)

EMPEROR: Phanocles—my dear, dear Phanocles! Be the first to congratulate me! It worked!

MAMILLIUS: Grandfather—what are we to do?

EMPEROR: Do, my dear boy? Make one in solid gold!

MAMILLIUS: About Postumus?

EMPEROR: Ah! The Heir Designate. I had put him out of my mind. We shall deal with Postumus presently. What a momentous discovery it was! I must sit....

MAMILLIUS: But, Grandfather—

EMPEROR: We shall bargain. A drink with you, Phanocles?

PHANOCLES: I shall drink no more. I am sane and I will die sane.

EMPEROR: Not enjoy what might be our last hour?

PHANOCLES: Humanity is mad, Caesar, or how could an Emperor be an old man who lives in a cloud of fantasy, and yet rules the world?

EMPEROR: What else is there in life but these conceptions that you call fantasy? Have at you, Phanocles!

PHANOCLES: I cannot debate.

EMPEROR: Life is a personal matter. Alexander did not fight his wars till I discovered him at the age of seven. When I was a baby, life was a single instant; but I pushed, bawled, saw, smelled, tasted, heard, that one point into whole palaces of history!

PHANOCLES: You say nothing.

EMPEROR: You do not choose to understand me. Do you think that your pressure cooker was for the satisfaction of a gross appetite? If I read a book now —say the Eclogues—I am not transported to a Roman Arcady; no. I become a boy, as I was when I first read it.

PHANOCLES: A poor return for reading.

57

EMPEROR: Do you think so? The most precious thing in life is a memory. When I tasted the fish from your cooker, I was aware on the instant of a hundred subtle perceptions that time has blunted; and, suddenly, it came back to me—I was young again! Yes—yes! I was lying above her. She was smooth and secret; she quivered, slightly. I was passionately alive—there was a sense of triumph, of domination, of power, of rape! I struck with lion's claws—she was out! She was mine. My first trout.

MAMILLIUS: Grandfather! For the last time—Are we to die and do nothing?

EMPEROR: Let us first drink a health, Mamillius. I give you —the pressure cooker! The most Promethean discovery of them all!

PHANOCLES: I cannot understand you, Caesar. You are not a fool, but you talk like one.

MAMILLIUS: This is the Emperor!

PHANOCLES: For the next hour.

MAMILLIUS: You are insolent!

PHANOCLES: We are going to die.

EMPEROR: Shall I be trite, Phanocles, and remind you that we were always going to die?

PHANOCLES: I had so many things to do. . . .

EMPEROR: Ah, yes—your toys. But your personal machinery —these levers and catapulting muscles—you did not think them indestructible?

PHANOCLES: Caesar, I conquered the universe, and yet the ants have defeated me. What is wrong with man?

EMPEROR: Men. A steam ship, or anything powerful, in the hands of man, Phanocles, is like a sharp knife in the hands of a child. There is nothing wrong with the knife. There is nothing wrong with the steam ship. There is nothing wrong with man's intelligence. The trouble is his nature.

MAMILLIUS: The last lesson.

PHANOCLES: Intelligence *is* the whole man. You are a fool after all, Caesar.

MAMILLIUS: You—you! dare to talk like—

EMPEROR: Be quiet, Mamillius. My friend has added to my life.

MAMILLIUS: Another insult like that, and I will subtract from his!

EMPEROR: The Imperial dignity is adequately safe-guarded in my hands. And now to our diplomacy.

MAMILLIUS: What is there to do?

EMPEROR: Negotiate.

MAMILLIUS: Using what?

EMPEROR: He has the men. We have the intelligence.

MAMILLIUS: Did you smile, Phanocles?

PHANOCLES: I, Lord?

MAMILLIUS: I thought you smiled. I am glad you did not smile, Phanocles. Forgive me, Grandfather—you were saying—?

EMPEROR: Let him negotiate from strength and he will make mistakes that will astonish you. People always under-estimate intelligence, do they not?

PHANOCLES: They do, Caesar.

(ENTER CAPTAIN.)

EMPEROR: Ah, Captain. You have come for the night pass-word?

CAPTAIN: No, Caesar. Excuse me, Caesar—

MAMILLIUS: Captain!

CAPTAIN: Sir?

MAMILLIUS: We are in danger.

CAPTAIN: It is true then, sir?

EMPEROR: Do not trouble yourself, Captain.

MAMILLIUS: The Father of his Country is in danger!

CAPTAIN: In defence of the Father of his Country I would—

MAMILLIUS: Could you defend the villa?

CAPTAIN: Sir, I could defend it to the death.

EMPEROR: What an astonishingly egotistical sentiment! Could you defend it successfully?

CAPTAIN: No, Caesar.

MAMILLIUS: Perhaps the Captain could find us a boat.

EMPEROR: Have you ever seen fugitives arrested in a boat? It

59

is perhaps the most degrading form of arrest. Consider. There is a swift boat—not yours, Phanocles. And there is a small boat—a dinghy. The fugitives row. They are inevitably overtaken. They cannot hide. They are forced at last to lie on their oars, and are finally loaded into the pursuing trireme like mules on a block and tackle. No, Mamillius. Let us not add to our humiliations by attempting to escape by boat. I have another use for the Captain.

CAPTAIN: Excuse me, sir—and Caesar. But—

MAMILLIUS: The Emperor has a command for you.

CAPTAIN: Yes, sir—but—

EMPEROR: Well, Captain?

CAPTAIN: The lady, sir.

MAMILLIUS: Euphrosyne!

CAPTAIN: I believe the lady is sister to the Director-General of Experimental Studies, Caesar?

EMPEROR: What of her?

CAPTAIN: She came to the guardroom, Caesar, in a state of great agitation—and she had such a tale to tell of rebellion—

EMPEROR: About Postumus?

CAPTAIN: Caesar, is it true that he—?

EMPEROR: Indeed it is.

CAPTAIN: In that case, Caesar, I wish to renew my assertion of loyalty.

EMPEROR: I am delighted, Captain. Provided we survive the day, I shall promote you so high that you will be quite dizzy.

MAMILLIUS: Where is the lady now?

EMPEROR: The main thing is that she is safe, Mamillius, and we shall send for her presently. Now, Captain, you must take a message from me to the Heir Designate. Tell him I have proposals to make. For example, the shift of power could be effected more easily in Rome, before the Senate. Tell him, Captain, that I am tired of ruling, but not of

living. Add that the presence of the Lord Mamillius would be essential.

CAPTAIN: Caesar!

MAMILLIUS: Is that all?

EMPEROR: Tell him, Captain, that we must meet once more,
before he does irreparable damage to his prospects
of an untroubled reign.

MAMILLIUS: What good would my presence do in Rome?

EMPEROR: Point out, Captain, that the presence of the Lord
Mamillius in demonstrable freedom would ensure
that my subjects understood that the proclamation
was made by me freely.

CAPTAIN: Caesar!

EMPEROR: Take the message as a Captain and bring back a
favourable reply as a Colonel.

CAPTAIN: Caesar! Yes, Caesar! But the lady, sir—she's
outside. . . .

MAMILLIUS: Euphrosyne!

EMPEROR: Allow the lady to pass.

CAPTAIN: Caesar! All right, lads—let her come in.
(ENTER EUPHROSYNE, *still in a dream*.)

EMPEROR: Child, where have you been? There is danger
everywhere but in the women's quarters.

EUPHROSYNE: I came back here earlier, Caesar, when the two
soldiers were talking to you. I stayed in that doorway long enough to know that a terrible thing had
been done and that you and my brother and the
young Lord were in great danger . . . and then . . .
something happened to me.

MAMILLIUS: Where did you go?

EUPHROSYNE: Down to the quay.

EMPEROR: My child, what possessed you? You took a very
grave risk. A young girl, like you, going off alone
—among all those soldiers!

EUPHROSYNE: There was no risk, Caesar—they would not think I
was going to hurt them. No one had eyes or
thoughts for any but the drowned or the dying.
There was no sign of my brother's ship—only

61

wreckage and smoke, and dead men lying in rows at the water's edge. . . .

MAMILLIUS: Oh, Euphrosyne—how terrible for you!

EUPHROSYNE: I felt nothing. They were like a *picture* of dead men . . . (*astonished*). Do you know, Mamillius, I could think of nothing but you—

MAMILLIUS: Do you love me so much?

EUPHROSYNE: Nothing but you. They were dead and dying—and —and yet I could only think of you! Oh, Mamillius! (*breaks down*).

MAMILLIUS: Grandfather—we love each other! Before we die, I want to marry her.

PHANOCLES: Impossible!

MAMILLIUS: What?

PHANOCLES: Tell him, Euphrosyne. We die today, and all vows are cancelled.

EUPHROSYNE: Must I?

MAMILLIUS: This is the moment for truth. What was your vow?

EUPHROSYNE: (*reciting*). "Not to engage in frivolous conversation with the ungodly; and not to reveal my transitory beauty to the eyes of pagan concupiscence."

MAMILLIUS: Of *what*?

EUPHROSYNE: (*repeating*). —of pagan concupiscence.

MAMILLIUS: Oh. . . . Pagan? Country people? Why should you fear them?

EMPEROR: It is simple, like all tragedy. She is a Christian.

MAMILLIUS: Is that all?

PHANOCLES: All? Do you know what General Postumus did to the Christians he found in Clusium? And do you know how I have been driven half across the Empire because she would not give up this superstitious nonsense? She is my ward. I am responsible in law—even for her beliefs.

MAMILLIUS: Let her believe what she will! You have me, too.

EUPHROSYNE: You are a prince.

MAMILLIUS: My throat is half-cut—what sort of a prince is that? Grandfather—*make* her marry me!

EMPEROR: She is a free woman in law, and technically a criminal. The situation is one of some complexity.

MAMILLIUS: Change the law, then!

EMPEROR: Have you forgotten Postumus and his approaching Fleet? The effect of a legal change would be purely local.

MAMILLIUS: The change I want is local. (*To* EUPHROSYNE) You love me. Will you change your religion for me?

EUPHROSYNE: No! Never!

MAMILLIUS: I loved you when you were nothing but a shape for my mind to play with. I loved you before I heard your voice or saw your face. In the same way, whatever comes, I will embrace the hidden future.

EMPEROR: Wait! Believe me, I should have no objection were the marriage private. I have found that Christians make bad philosophers, but good civil servants. I see no reason why a Christian should not make an excellent wife.

EUPHROSYNE: Caesar, forgive me! You do not understand. He is a part of the world that is forbidden me. We Christians must re-make the world. It is a condition of our belief. I cannot say "Yes". You are a pagan—a believer in the old gods—

MAMILLIUS: But I do not believe in the old gods!

PHANOCLES: No intelligent man believes in them!

EMPEROR: But there remains something, nevertheless. We—they—do not believe in Jupiter, Phanocles, but it is a condition of our existence that we should pretend to believe. A pretended belief is better than a belief in nothing at all.

PHANOCLES: No!

EMPEROR: Surely!

PHANOCLES: And there is always something to believe in, Caesar. I give you the names of my new gods: Law, Change, Cause and Effect, Reason—and

63

Reason is the greatest. You could have those gods in place of the old ones.

EMPEROR: You know, Mamillius, I suspect that Phanocles will survive us all. His gods and those of General Postumus are too alike to quarrel!

MAMILLIUS: Tell me about your gods, Euphrosyne. Do they sound as cold as his?

EUPHROSYNE: There is only one God.

MAMILLIUS: Can he save us, do you think, from those ships?

EUPHROSYNE: If it is His will.

MAMILLIUS: If it *should* be his will, he's leaving it rather late. The first of the ships is coming in to the quay. Postumus must be itching to hurl your explosive at us, Phanocles. What will happen? Shall we all be killed?

PHANOCLES: No, Lord. It could not reach the villa.

MAMILLIUS: Are you sure?

PHANOCLES: I am sure. At worst a hole in the cliff face some yards below where you are standing.

MAMILLIUS: I suppose he *will* let loose the thing?

EMPEROR: He could hardly resist it. But not until he has a good audience.

MAMILLIUS: And what then?

EMPEROR: Assuming that our worthy Phanocles knows what he is talking about, then at least we ought all to be alive after his device has tunnelled into our cliffs. Our best hope then lies in the message I sent with the Captain. Postumus delights in telling us he is a realist who takes no chances. We must somehow persuade him that he is taking no chances by allowing you to live, Mamillius.

MAMILLIUS: I will not cringe to him, Grandfather!

EMPEROR: No, I can see that you will not. Euphrosyne, I fear I must hold you largely responsible for an astonishing change in my grandson— a change which deserves life—not death. He will listen to you. What do you advise?

EUPHROSYNE: Pray.

64

MAMILLIUS: How? To what?

EUPHROSYNE: To God.

EMPEROR: Ah, but which god? You mean *your* God?

EUPHROSYNE: What else?

MAMILLIUS: Then you pray, Euphrosyne! No god could refuse a prayer from you!

EUPHROSYNE: I dare not. But He elects whom He will—or so they said. . . .

MAMILLIUS: Pray, dear Euphrosyne—for love of me!

EUPHROSYNE: I love you, whatever happens. If it is a sin to love a pagan, then I will pay for it gladly!

MAMILLIUS: And I love you! We should have found out about each other—spent our lives—open towards each other, like a couple of friendly cupboards. . . . My goods should be your goods, my house your house—my life your life!

EUPHROSYNE: I have nothing to give in exchange.

MAMILLIUS: Yourself!

EUPHROSYNE: I had nothing but my God. . . .

MAMILLIUS: I will share your gods!

EUPHROSYNE: If only you could!

MAMILLIUS: If you believe, that is enough for me. Your gods shall be my gods!

EUPHROSYNE: My *God* shall be thy God.

MAMILLIUS: Very well. Thy *God* shall be my God. Kiss me. (*They embrace.*)

EMPEROR: Bless you, my children. Because of that wretched man down there I have not the heart to make a longer speech. I should have enjoyed your happiness. . . .

MAMILLIUS: (*The man of action*). Grandfather—pray!

EMPEROR: Since you propose to be a Christian, Mamillius, it would be better if you did.

MAMILLIUS: But how? Euphrosyne. . . .

EUPHROSYNE: No. . . .

EMPEROR: (*philosophically*). Yes, Euphrosyne. He is right. Prayer is an admission of human frailty, and therefore, though we may not believe in the object of our prayer, we should at least make the admission. To whom shall we pray?

EUPHROSYNE: To whom but God?

EMPEROR: Ah, yes, of course. You have no difficulty there, have you? A womanish answer—but excusable in the circumstances.

MAMILLIUS: Grandfather—you are Jupiter's High Pontiff.

EMPEROR: Well . . . yes.

MAMILLIUS: Hurry, Grandfather—pray!

EMPEROR: My dear boy! To think I should have to wait until now to find out that you are fundamentally religious! Very well. Let us accept our probable defeat with the usual dignified forms. Stand, Phanocles.

PHANOCLES: (*as in a daze*). Caesar, I named *my* god. Reason.

EMPEROR: I think we have enough gods for the moment. Stand, Phanocles.

PHANOCLES: Reason might have shown us a way. If only I had trusted and invoked—

MAMILLIUS: (*fierce*). If you will not stand for Jupiter, Phanocles, perhaps you will do so for the Emperor.

PHANOCLES: (*stands*). Caesar!

EMPEROR: Bring me the bowl, Mamillius. Now the lamp. Should you be doing this? I think not. Phanocles, place the lamp on the table—Incense. . . .

MAMILLIUS: (*whispering to the kneeling* EUPHROSYNE). Are you praying, Euphrosyne?

EUPHROSYNE: When I *saw* them—they were like a picture—yet why when I only *think* of them should they appear so terrible? We must pray for God's mercy on the dying!

MAMILLIUS: But that's not the point. I want *us* to live!

EUPHROSYNE: (*with a look of appeal*). Try, dear Mamillius—try to pray! He is the God of Love!

EMPEROR: (*busy with his rituals, quietly to* PHANOCLES). See, Phanocles—that is always the way with a young religion. I have no doubt that Christianity will achieve a formal etiquette in time, like all the

66

others. . . . Incense, Phanocles. Pour water over my hands. (PHANOCLES *does so.*) Gently, Phanocles. The washing is symbolic only. (*He finishes.*)
(MAMILLIUS'S *attention is uncertainly divided between* EUPHROSYNE *and the* EMPEROR *and his own efforts at silent prayer.*)
Are we all ready? (*Pause*) Be absent every un-propitious speech. Let every unhallowed tongue keep silent! (*Tense pause*) All Father. . . .

PHANOCLES: (*in a great shout*) Great Caesar! Forgive me for a fool! Reason *is* the only god!
(*A short tense silence*)

EMPEROR: I doubt if your madness can excuse sacrilege, Phanocles.

PHANOCLES: But the brass butterfly. . . . Think. . . . We could force Postumus to destroy himself by his own hand! . . .
(MAMILLIUS, *noticing that* EUPHROSYNE *has stopped praying and is greatly upset, seizes his sword, and rushes to* PHANOCLES.)

MAMILLIUS: I swear I'll kill you if you make another sound!
(PHANOCLES *succumbs.*)

EMPEROR: Let him be, Mamillius. He is calm now. I am familiar with the convulsions of religious hysteria and I can see the fit has passed. Phanocles, I promise you that in a few moments you may in-voke your god of Reason to your heart's content, but we must give precedence to Jupiter. In the circumstances, Mamillius, do you mind officiating once more? We need only repeat the symbolic washing. . . . (MAMILLIUS *pours water.*) Now, are we all ready?
Great Jupiter, All Father, Lord of heaven and earth, accept this sacrifice from us and hear our prayer. Oh, Conductor of Souls, deliver us from danger! Oh, Lord of the Lightning, Thunderer, destroy our enemies!
(*There is a fearful and reverberating explosion.*

THE EMPEROR *is transfixed.*

EUPHROSYNE *gives a cry and is also transfixed. Indeed, they are all more or less transfixed.*)

MAMILLIUS: Thunder! Grandfather! was it on the right hand? Grandfather—there's something wrong—you prayed to Jupiter! There is nothing down there but smoke—I can't see anything—(*looking towards* EUPHROSYNE). A miracle! But whose miracle?

PHANOCLES: No, no, no, no, no!

MAMILLIUS: I can see now—that is where the soldiers were standing, but they've all gone! The hedges over the quay are burning—

PHANOCLES: Impossible! The firing mechanism was foolproof—unless someone removed the—

(MAMILLIUS *leaves the wall and runs to* EUPHROSYNE.)

MAMILLIUS: Euphrosyne, my love—we are saved! Jupiter has destroyed our enemies!

EUPHROSYNE: It was our God! He guided my hand—

MAMILLIUS: (*incredulous*). The God of Love?—Striking people with lightning?

EUPHROSYNE: But He is the God of Battles, too!

EMPEROR: Not a cloud. Not a cloud anywhere. . . .

MAMILLIUS: (*triumphant*). Abandon Jupiter, Grandfather! Grandfather—did you hear? Love and War at one altar! This is comprehensive!

(*He returns happily to the cliff wall.*

During the ensuing dialogue EUPHROSYNE *takes the brass butterfly from her dress and holds it close to her breast in terror.*)

Why! The statue of Hercules is lying down in pieces by the pedestal! And the trees—how peculiar. . . . The smoke has almost cleared. . . . But there's nobody about—and where are the steps—and the boats that were tied up alongside them?

PHANOCLES: It could never happen, Caesar. I made certain!

MAMILLIUS: Some of the trees are down, and some are leaning against the others. . . .

PHANOCLES: (*to himself*). The only possible explanation!

MAMILLIUS: There's a man running—

PHANOCLES: Some fool removed it—

MAMILLIUS: Grandfather, a man is coming up the steps to the villa, running—

EMPEROR: Are there any clouds?

MAMILLIUS: Not a cloud in the sky! Only smoke down by the quay—

PHANOCLES: Yet who—*who* would have tampered with it? What fool—?

MAMILLIUS: I seem to know him—

PHANOCLES: (*to* MAMILLIUS)—unless the Heir Designate himself—

MAMILLIUS: No, it's certainly not Postumus—Why, he's our Captain.

PHANOCLES: I am not a vengeful man, but that would be a sort of justice—

MAMILLIUS: Phanocles! You *can* smile!

(*We begin to see in* PHANOCLES *the effect of a grim joke dawning on him.*)

PHANOCLES: The Heir Designate himself!

MAMILLIUS: —but it's not! It's our Captain. He'll tell us what happened!

PHANOCLES: (*still savouring his private thought*). At least only he could have ordered its removal . . . (*a hollow chuckle*). Divine retribution!

MAMILLIUS: (*waving*). Captain! Captain!

PHANOCLES: (*surveying all three compassionately*). How can they *not* believe in gods!

(ENTER CAPTAIN.)

CAPTAIN: Caesar! I tried to give your message to the Heir Designate—but I was prevented. And now he's dead, Caesar—they are all dead, or dying—

EMPEROR: Who—is—dead?

CAPTAIN: General Postumus, the Heir Designate, Caesar!

EMPEROR: The Heir Designate?

CAPTAIN: —and his officers, Caesar. It was . . . well, I hardly like to say this. There's nothing in the regulations to go by—It was a miracle—an Act of God—

EMPEROR: God?

CAPTAIN: The All Father—praised be his name! The Thunderer—Jupiter. . . . I must start from the beginning —They were all standing by the Mark Seven and laughing, Caesar. The lamented General was bending down to loose the rachet; and then there was a kind of a sort of—there was a kind of white bang, Caesar, and a storm of smoke billowing out. They went to pieces—and in the middle of them the lamented General passed on, leaving nothing behind him but his helmet, which fell on the south wing of the villa. There's nothing left of the distinguished officers who followed him, Caesar. As for the quay, Caesar—there's a smoking hole where the quay was!
(LONG *pause*)

EMPEROR: Captain, go down to the misguided and—irreligious soldiers who are coming in to the quay. Tell them that Jupiter, the All Father, has destroyed the Heir Designate before their very eyes, for the sin of open rebellion against the Emperor.

CAPTAIN: Caesar! (*Pause*) Hail, Caesar!
(EXIT CAPTAIN.

EUPHROSYNE *swoons. The brass arming vane falls from her hand.* MAMILLIUS *picks her up and comforts her.*

PHANOCLES *rushes forward, grabs the arming vane.*)

MAMILLIUS: Euphrosyne, my love, did you hear? It is as I said —we have all our lives. Jupiter—I mean our God —has protected us. We have nothing more to fear!
(EUPHROSYNE *has opened her eyes. She smiles—then sees* PHANOCLES *standing, rooted, over her and holding the brass butterfly.*)

PHANOCLES: My intelligent sister. . . . This was exactly calculated! We owe our lives—

EUPHROSYNE: No, Phanocles—no! I was guided in all I did. It was like a dream. . . . I had no fear, no doubts. . . . I did not even try to hide—all those dead men

70

were nothing to do with me. God killed them!

MAMILLIUS: What is that, Phanocles?

PHANOCLES: The arming vane, Lord—what I was trying to explain—

MAMILLIUS: How did she get it?

PHANOCLES: God knows!

(EUPHROSYNE *is on the verge of happy tears as* MAMILLIUS *takes her in his arms.*)

What did I tell you, Caesar? Here is the brass butterfly—the safeguard!

EMPEROR: (*miles away*). I must adjust my conception of the universe. . . .

MAMILLIUS: Dry your tears. Look up. The sun has risen for us.

PHANOCLES: She took it off, so of course the weapon would have to explode as soon as he fired it!

EMPEROR: It is perhaps natural that the All Father should take especial care of his own High Pontiff—but he's never done it before!

PHANOCLES: So you see, Cause and Effect still holds good, Caesar.

EMPEROR: (*at last focusing on* PHANOCLES). And you, Phanocles—you with your talk of Law and Change and Reason—you dared to suggest that the universe is a machine!

PHANOCLES: But look, Caesar! I have just been telling you—

EMPEROR: You can tell me nothing more. Where is all your logic when the gods take a hand?

PHANOCLES: I . . . I don't know.

EMPEROR: We were helpless—condemned to death—with only a glimmer of hope. Yet, out of this limpid sky, his lightning struck your machine, and the elect were elected.

PHANOCLES: I . . . Yes, Caesar. (*He is defeated.*)

EUPHROSYNE: (*happy now*). Never let me go!

MAMILLIUS: How could I? Keep looking at me!

EUPHROSYNE: Where else should I look?

EMPEROR: Mamillius—

MAMILLIUS: Grandfather?

EMPEROR: They are right after all.

MAMILLIUS: Who?

EMPEROR: Just they. The simple, the old wives. The mad philosophers and the frantic priests—even the savage in the desert with his piece of wood. They are right after all. And I was wrong. Hopelessly wrong—Postumus spoke more truly than he knew. It is time for a regency.

MAMILLIUS: Grandfather!

EMPEROR: Yes?

MAMILLIUS: Postumus is dead. Who is the next Heir Designate?

EMPEROR: Who but you?

MAMILLIUS: Caesar!

EMPEROR: Any man can bring about a change—and yet change is the one thing no man can control. Therefore, Mamillius, ruling is necessary, but nonsense. You will make a terrible Emperor—What does that matter since the gods take a hand?

MAMILLIUS: I shall be the greatest of Emperors!

EMPEROR: Do not remind me too soon of my folly!

MAMILLIUS: —with the Empress Euphrosyne beside me—

EMPEROR: I forgot—stop—stop!

MAMILLIUS: No, Grandfather, you cannot control us any more than you can control change. Her god may or may not strike out of a clear sky, but he is *her* God, and her God shall be my God. I have sworn it. Come with me, my Empress Designate!

EMPEROR: Wait!

MAMILLIUS: What for, Grandfather?

EUPHROSYNE: To receive his blessing, Mamillius. We are right after all. By trusting love we trusted God. Isn't that what you meant?

EMPEROR: Did I?

EUPHROSYNE: Oh, but you made everything so clear! There is a time for weeping, a time for rejoicing, and a time to marry. How simple life is after all!

EMPEROR: Do you mean to marry my grandson?

EUPHROSYNE: I do!

EMPEROR: And you, Mamillius?

MAMILLIUS: I do, I do!

EMPEROR: If my blessing means taking my love with you into the future, then you are blessed already. But the thought of that future is strangely oppressive.

MAMILLIUS: But why, Grandfather? The future is ours now. You have seen to that, and we are eager to alter it together.

EMPEROR: That is what oppresses me. I must seek guidance; though goodness knows where! Leave me now and come back in an hour.

MAMILLIUS: Thank you Grandfather. Hail and—for an hour—farewell, Caesar! Come, Euphrosyne.

EUPHROSYNE: (*Kisses the Emperor, then steps back. She speaks with intense emotion.*)
God save our gracious Emperor!

MAMILLIUS: Do you really love me?

EUPHROSYNE: I told you so.

MAMILLIUS: Say it again!

EUPHROSYNE: I do, I do, I do!

EMPEROR: Wait, I beg of you, Mamillius!

MAMILLIUS: No, Grandfather—no, no, no! Hail, and for a little while—farewell, Caesar! Now, where were we? Oh yes—(*to* EUPHROSYNE) Tell me, do you really and truly love me? . . .
(*They have gone.*)

EMPEROR: This is the end in every direction.

PHANOCLES: But we are saved! Now we can go on! The obstacles have been removed by, by—

EMPEROR: The All Father.

PHANOCLES: We can build ourselves a bigger steamship, Caesar.
(THE EMPEROR *begins to get angry. The day's trans-actions have left their mark. There is an unwonted readiness in his anger and later, in both anger and excitement, a touch of hysteria.*)

EMPEROR: A bigger steamship! Phanocles, son of Myron,

73

Director-General of Experimental Studies—did
you hear what he said?

PHANOCLES: She is only a girl.

EMPEROR: Clever man, learned man, genius—what a fool
you are!

PHANOCLES: I?

EMPEROR: There is no death hanging over them other than
the one that waits us all—her God *shall* be his God!
He means it and she means it—and what is an
Empire to a pretty girl?

PHANOCLES: But Caesar—

EMPEROR: Do you see what you have done?

PHANOCLES: I have done nothing.

EMPEROR: You did nothing! A steamship that wrecks half a
fleet—an explosive that claps out half an army—
and now—now—just when the All Father is
pleased to signify his personal interest in the
succession—*now!* A Christian Emperor!

PHANOCLES: It is not my fault that she is a Christian!

EMPEROR: Why did you come here?

PHANOCLES: To see you.

EMPEROR: Can you control the elements and not your own
sister? What have I done that at my age I should
be forced to suffer like this?

PHANOCLES: When you are used to my inventions, Caesar, the
old world will seem like an evil dream.

EMPEROR: But I like the old world! What has yours to offer?
A white bang! Wheels like sharks' teeth! Unrest,
ferment, fever, dislocation, disorder, wild experiment and catastrophe!

(THE EMPEROR *almost feels his way to a seat and
lowers himself into it.*)

This is a delirium!

PHANOCLES: Shall I call your physician?

EMPEROR: Have we dreamed, Phanocles? Are you my in-
digestion?

PHANOCLES: No.

EMPEROR: Let me . . . experiment. This feels like a cup, and

74

you see that though my hand shakes, I can pour straight. Delusions, destruction, ruin, flames, a divine intervention—steamships and clapper-outers. . . .

PHANOCLES: Caesar—Caesar! Do you feel better, Caesar?

EMPEROR: Better. Sadder. Wiser. Bang. Boom.

PHANOCLES: Caesar. . . . The—the pressure cooker. . . . Nyum, nyum!

EMPEROR: The Promethean pressure cooker—

PHANOCLES: Trout.

EMPEROR: Levels of shining water and cataracts from the dark rock on high. Music! Just the harp. . . .
(MUSIC) (*Pause*)
The old world returns to me—the old world which is this world. Of course. . . . There is no other.

PHANOCLES: Trout, Caesar. . . .

EMPEROR: This libation to the Thunderer—

PHANOCLES: Think of the pressure cooker—

EMPEROR: I am myself again. Well, Phanocles—how am I to reward you?

PHANOCLES: As Caesar will. I was certain that in the long run you would see the sense of my inventions, Caesar.

EMPEROR: I shall have one made in pure gold. Or would silver be more suitable? There is an excellent field for your ingenuity, my dear Director-General.

PHANOCLES: Perhaps access to more workmen and a bigger boat—

EMPEROR: Who was talking about boats?

PHANOCLES: She was so fast. . . .

EMPEROR: Blasphemously so!

PHANOCLES: Have you no use for a fast boat, Caesar?

EMPEROR: You will say I am old—but I prefer a slow boat. We will have nothing but slow boats in future.

PHANOCLES: But Caesar!

EMPEROR: Besides, have you considered how unfair she was to the slaves?

PHANOCLES: She would have made them unnecessary.

EMPEROR: Well, there you are, you see. To be a slave-rower is a hard life, Phanocles, but it is better than no life at all. You do not have to think of these things, but I am responsible for the well-being of all classes. Your fast boats would lead to nothing but a pool of unemployment, and I am not hard-hearted enough to countenance that.

PHANOCLES: There is work enough in a steamship—

EMPEROR: Besides, you cannot find your way without a wind when the stars or the sun are hidden.

PHANOCLES: I had thought of an instrument that points to the North.

EMPEROR: What would be the use of that? No one wants to go there.

PHANOCLES: You have not thought—

EMPEROR: For the future nothing but slow boats. It is Our Imperial Will, Phanocles.

PHANOCLES: I bow.

EMPEROR: Whatever else we do, we must look after the slaves. They are a sacred charge.

PHANOCLES: Perhaps one day, Caesar, when men are free because they no longer believe themselves to be slaves—

EMPEROR: You work among perfect elements, and therefore politically you are an idealist. There will always be slaves, though the name may change. What is slavery but the domination of the weak by the strong? How can you make them equal? Or are you fool enough to think they are born equal?

PHANOCLES: My explosive makes the strong weak.

EMPEROR: Your explosive is even more unsettling than your ship. Certainly it has—under Jupiter—preserved me this day, and therefore the peace of the Empire. But it has cost the world a merciless ruler who would have murdered half a dozen people and given justice to a hundred million. The world has lost a bargain. No, Phanocles. No more explosives. . . . Your pressure cooker. . . . I shall reward you for that.

PHANOCLES: Caesar—you will reward me well for this—

EMPEROR: For what?

PHANOCLES: You remember the third great invention I was keeping in reserve to surprise you? Here it is.

EMPEROR: Careful, Phanocles! Put it down! Put it down, I said!

PHANOCLES: But Caesar—

EMPEROR: Keep off!

PHANOCLES: There is nothing to fear. Look, Caesar—touch if you will.

EMPEROR: Nothing about vapour—no steam—no noise?

PHANOCLES: Now, how will you reward me?

EMPEROR: It has no connection with—(*pointing up*).

PHANOCLES: With silence only. Look.

EMPEROR: I see nothing but two pieces of paper.

PHANOCLES: Take them.

EMPEROR: Poems? You are a poet? That is quite incredible!

PHANOCLES: Mamillius wrote the lines.

EMPEROR: I might have known! Sophocles—Aeschylus— How well read the boy is!

PHANOCLES: This will make him famous. Read both papers, Caesar, for they are exactly the same. I have invented a cheap and noiseless method of multiplying books. I call it printing.

EMPEROR: Printing?

PHANOCLES: Think. How many books of mathematics are irretrievably lost that this invention would have saved for us? How much astronomy, medicine if you will —husbandry, essential skills—

EMPEROR: But this is another pressure cooker!

PHANOCLES: By this method a man and a boy could make a thousand copies of a book in a day.

EMPEROR: We could give away a hundred thousand copies of the works of Homer!

PHANOCLES: A million if you will.

EMPEROR: A poet will sell his verses by the sack, like

vegetables—"Buy my fine ripe odes!" (*He is really excited.*)

PHANOCLES: A public library in every town!

EMPEROR: Phanocles—dear Phanocles! Perhaps the world is not too old to learn. Ten thousand copies of the love poems of Catullus!

PHANOCLES: A hundred thousand of the works of Mamillius—

EMPEROR: Encyclopaedias!

PHANOCLES: An author in every street, Caesar! We shall set man free by liberating his frustrated desire for self-expression.

EMPEROR: Self-expression! (*he is suddenly cautious*). Was that the first cool breeze of evening I felt on my neck? Phanocles, let us be very careful. Let us assess this invention of yours *before* it claps out—

PHANOCLES: How can printing clap-out?

EMPEROR: Self-expression. Is there genius enough to go round?

PHANOCLES: Let history convince you, Caesar. In our library at Alexandria there are more books than a man could read in seven lifetimes.

EMPEROR: That would seem to suggest that we have more than enough books already. How often is a Horace born?

PHANOCLES: Come, Caesar—nature is bountiful.

EMPEROR: But supposing we all write books? Each man will be lured to erect himself a small but indelible monument—

PHANOCLES: Interesting biographies—

EMPEROR: Diary of a Provincial Governor. . . . I built Hadrian's Wall. . . .

PHANOCLES: Scholarship, then—

EMPEROR: Books about books about books—

PHANOCLES: History—

EMPEROR: Can you not understand, extraordinary man? A great historian is born less frequently than a great poet! But every man who is indeed so frightened of the future that he can think only of the past

78

will labour at the bald outline. And every person who thinks his own life of cosmic importance will give us a blow by by blow description of the fight. I was Nero's Grandmother. I was Nursey to the little Prince Mamillius—

PHANOCLES: I see a new heaven and a new earth! The masses of information will grow, will swell, will become a torrent. There will be corridors and quarries of books—pillars and pyramids of them!

EMPEROR: The ceilings will lift, will burst—

PHANOCLES: Reports, Caesar—a stream of ceaseless facts!

EMPEROR: Reports! Who will read them? Not you! I shall read them. Reports—military, naval, sanitary—I shall have to read them all! Political, statistical, economical, theological—(*pause*). Let my eunuch sing to me again. . . .

(THE EUNUCH *sings.* THE EMPEROR *touches a pillar, observes what is now the exquisite beauty of the night.*

A WOMAN *is lighting the lamps. The music, the stars, the pools of light, calm them. The play is fading now, slowly and gently as the day has done.*)
Forgive me, Phanocles—

PHANOCLES: What is there to forgive, Caesar? You have done nothing.

EMPEROR: I touched that factual stone to exorcise the vision. I am too old for these terrors. . . .

PHANOCLES: Terrors, Caesar?

EMPEROR: The vistas you show me are too magnificent.

PHANOCLES: I see no vistas and I feel no terrors.

EMPEROR: Of course. You are a force of nature, Phanocles—not solely a man. There is no stopping you. I can only divert you. For you will continue invincibly exercising your partial foresight till your inventor pulls out the pin and your mechanism jolts to a stop.

PHANOCLES: You mean when I die.

EMPEROR: How exquisite beyond expression is the beauty of

the common world! Will you rub it away, I
wonder, as I rub the bloom from this grape?

PHANOCLES: I should change it.

EMPEROR: But to please me—as a wedding present for your
sister—you would not consent to let that frantic
brain of yours occupy itself with, say, gardening?

PHANOCLES: Why not, Caesar? I have often thought that the
yield of the earth is scandalously low. I have con-
ceived a number of contrivances—

EMPEROR: I understand you, indomitable man. Well,
Phanocles, I shall reward you for the pressure
cooker.

PHANOCLES: I am in Caesar's hands.

EMPEROR: Would you care to be an ambassador?

PHANOCLES: My fondest dream has never reached to such a
position of distinction, Caesar! I should be your
representative in person!

EMPEROR: It would be rather a long journey, but of great
interest to an enquiring spirit such as your own.
Come, let us stroll together in the cool night air.
Yes. . . . You can take your explosive and your
printing with you. I shall make you Envoy
Extraordinary and Plenipotentiary. Phanocles, my
dear friend—I want you to take a *slow* boat to
China. . . .

(CURTAIN)